OBSERVING ACTIVITIES

Susan Cavendish is a lecturer and research associate at the School of Education, University of Leicester. She taught for several years before becoming involved in the ORACLE Groupwork and the STAR research projects. She is presently working on the Rural Schools Curriculum Enhancement National Evaluation Project and lectures in primary mathematics and science on the PGCE course.

Maurice Galton is director of the School of Education, University of Leicester. He has led a number of studies of primary schools including ORACLE (Observational Research and Classroom Learning Evaluation), Effective Groupwork in the Primary Classroom, PRISMS (Educational Provision in Small Primary Schools) and the Primary STAR (Science Teaching Action Research) project. He is presently involved in SCENE (Rural Schools Curriculum Enhancement National Evaluation Project).

Linda Hargreaves was educated at the University of Durham where she graduated with BSc in psychology in 1971. After teaching in Leicestershire infant and junior schools she gained an MA (Ed) at Leicester University in 1979. She designed a context-based assessment project on study skills for the project based at Leicester University School of Education, before joining the STAR project.

After graduating in physics at Oxford, **Wynne Harlen** taught in schools and colleges for a number of years before moving into research and curriculum development in primary science. She was engaged in the evaluation of, first the Oxford Primary Science project and then Science 5/13, at Bristol University from 1966 to 1973, gaining a PhD through research into evaluation procedures. For the next four years at Reading University, she led the Progress in Learning Science project which produced the 'Match and Mismatch' materials. During this time she edited *Evaluation and the Teacher's Role* for the Schools' Council and contributed to a number of other publications on curriculum evaluation, including *Values and Evaluation* and *Evaluation Roles*. She moved to London University in 1977 to what is now King's College, where she was deputy director of the APU science project, until her appointment in January 1985 as Sidney Jones Professor of Science Education at the University of Liverpool.

OBSERVING ACTIVITIES

SUSAN CAVENDISH, MAURICE GALTON,
LINDA HARGREAVES and WYNNE HARLEN

P·C·P
Paul Chapman
Publishing Ltd

Paul Chapman Publishing Ltd
144 Liverpool Road
London
N1 1LA

British Library Cataloguing in Publication Data
Observing activities.
    1. England. Primary schools. Curriculum subjects:
    Science. Academic achievement of students. Assessment
    I. Cavendish, Susan   II. Series
    372.35

    ISBN 1-85396-076-4

Typeset by DP Photosetting, Aylesbury, Bucks
Printed by St Edmundsbury Press, Bury St Edmunds, England
Bound by W.H. Ware, Clevedon, Avon

A B C D E F 5 4 3 2 1 0

Contents

General introduction to the STAR series

During the past decade, increasing attention has been paid to the provision of science in the primary school. The desire to improve the quality of this provision has been a feature not only of the educational debate in the United Kingdom but also in other industrialized countries. It is, for example, the major focus of the Council of Europe's current educational programme. This attention stems largely from the realization that today's primary children need to be more 'scientifically literate' than previous generations were, if they are to solve the problems which will face them when they enter the world of work in the twenty-first century. The provision of Educational Support Grants (ESG) to local authorities and the elevation of science as a core curriculum area in the National Curriculum both illustrate the Government's determination to improve the quality of science teaching in our schools.

Earlier attempts to improve the provision of science in the primary school gave rise to large-scale projects funded by the then Schools Council. This approach was too simplistic, particularly in the assumption made about the willingness of teachers to commit themselves to changes which they themselves did not help to create. More recently school-focused curriculum research has tried to remedy this deficiency. However, the pragmatic approach generally adopted has made it difficult to transfer the practice developed within one school to others who did not participate in the original development.

The Science Teacher Action Research (STAR) project has tried to combine the advantages of 'project based' and 'school-focused curriculum development' approaches. While the STAR team provided a conceptual framework for teaching science at primary level, the application of this framework, in the form of tasks that were appropriate for children of different abilities and ages, was left to the teachers who participated in the project. It was hoped that the teaching of primary science, in this way, while informed by theory would also be practical. A key element in this strategy was to provide participating teachers with appropriate means of assessing pupil performance in different aspects of the scientific processes. While the close association between what is taught and what is assessed has long been recognized, it is only recently that the positive aspects of this relationship have been appreciated. Assessment procedures which reflect the objectives of the curriculum, not only tend to ensure closer correspondence between the intentions of those who develop the curriculum and the observed practice of those who implement it but also provide a common language, based on shared understandings of the learning processes involved. Such 'shared understandings' were essential in the STAR project if the participating teachers were to play a full part in its development.

As is now generally recognized, no one method of assessment enjoys sufficient advantages over others to ensure its exclusive use. Reliable judgements of pupil performance need to take into account the capacity of children to achieve in a variety of contexts. In the STAR project, attention was given to the performance of pupils on written tasks, during practical activities and in the context of general classroom work where teachers carried out systematic observation as part of their general monitoring procedure. Each of these approaches yields information which can be entered into a profile of pupil achievement, combining the advantages and minimizing the disadvantages of each respective method.

The STAR project team was based at the School of Education in Liverpool and Leicester. The work began in 1986 and was completed in September 1989. This second book is devoted to ways in which teachers can observe children during science activities and how such observations can be used as part of an overall assessment policy. As with the Walled Garden, the subject of the first volume, the construction of the observation schedule used in this study was a co-operative effort between the two institutions. The categories of the observation schedule were developed by Wynne Harlen at an earlier stage as part of an INSET course for primary teachers. In the original version several observers were required and expertise developed at Leicester during the ORACLE project was then used to refine this system so that it was capable of being used by a single observer. Subsequently the system was further refined by teachers taking part in the project so that it could be used under typical classroom conditions. Although the context in which this development took place was a scientific one these procedures can be applied to other areas of the curriculum. We hope, therefore, that it will serve a useful purpose for all who work in primary schools.

Maurice Galton and Wynne Harlen
Series Editors

Preface

The observation system, Science Process Observation Categories (SPOC), described in this book was developed for use in the Primary Science Teaching Action Research (STAR) project. The project was funded by the Leverhulme Trust and based jointly at the School of Education, Leicester University, and the Centre for Research in Primary Science and Technology in the Department of Education, Liverpool University, from January 1986 to September 1989.

The aim of the project was to identify good practice in the primary classroom, and to facilitate the formulation of strategies for improving the use of science process skills by children. Methods of in-service training for the sharing of expertise was also a major issue for the project.

Examination of children's skills involved collecting evidence from structured written and practical work, as well as from observations of children participating in normal classroom activities. These three aspects of assessment form the basis for the three books in the series titled 'Assessing Science in the Primary Classroom'. The SPOC observation system was employed by the project not only as an aid to the assessment of children, but also to provide information relating to the opportunity provided children for hypothesizing, interpreting, observing, etc. This book is based on the information provided by SPOC.

The change in science practice was brought about by the direct involvement of teachers, working collaboratively, in forming strategies, trying them out, and evaluating their effect. Sharing is viewed as of great importance by the STAR team, and this book is intended to share the STAR members' experiences with its readers, in particular teachers, advisers and in-service providers.

THE RESEARCH TEAM

The team worked from two centres:

at the School of Education, Leicester University – Susan Cavendish and Linda Hargreaves;

at the Centre for Research in Primary Science and Technology in the Department of Education, Liverpool University – Terry Russell and Mike Schilling;

with the joint directors of the project, Professors Maurice Galton and Wynne Harlen at Leicester and Liverpool respectively.

ACKNOWLEDGEMENTS

We should like to acknowledge the involvement and support of Cheshire, Leicester, Sheffield and Wirral Education Authorities and the encouragement given by the local authority education advisers. We are indebted to the advisory teacher teams who made the observation possible and would like to acknowledge the commitment and work of:

Keith Roberts (1986–7)
Roger Walker (1986–7)
Gerry Phillips (1986–7)   (Cheshire)
Annette Drake (1987–9)

Sue Eland
Geoff Tite   (Leicestershire)

Linda Gatens   (Sheffield)

Di Sutton
Elaine Weatherhead   (Wirral)

In particular, we wish to acknowledge the help of Bob Morley for his work with the Leicestershire teachers in developing their observation skills and we are indebted to all the teachers involved in the project for their valuable contributions. We also acknowledge Jaya Katariya for her endless patience in entering the observation data onto computer.

1

The Role of Process Skills in Learning Science

The best starting point for discussing learning in science and the role of process skills in it is to consider an example of learning in which process skills play a part.

A class of six year olds was exploring examples of water evaporating. They carried out various activities which enabled them to observe the phenomenon closely, such as washing clothes and hanging them up outside. They also monitored the level of water in a fish tank, making the changes evident by sticking on the tank a strip of paper with horizontal coloured bars marked on it and noting at which colour the surface was at different times.

After observations had been made of the change in the water level for some time, the teacher asked the children to draw and talk about their ideas about where the water had gone. There were a number of different explanations: 'the sun sucks it up' (accompanying a drawing of the sun with a drinking straw leading down to the tank); 'the water dried at the bottom of the bowl'; 'there is a little hole in the bowl'.

With the teacher's help, the children set about testing their ideas. The consideration of the possibility of a hole in the bottom of the tank led to the following activities. The teacher lifted up the tank for the children to look underneath and to feel with their hands if it was wet. Having found no hole the children wanted to check the joins at the edges of the tank. They decided to fill the tank up and to look later to see if any water had come out.

One child was concerned that the water might come out and then 'dry up' before they checked. So they decided to leave some 'control' drops beside the tank. If these drops were still present when they came to check the tank, then it was felt that any water that had leaked from the tank would also still be there. The children checked later, found the control drops still there but the table under the tank dry, so they were happy that no water was leaking out. They then proceeded to test the effect of the sun.

(Based on a case study collected
by the SPACE project, 1989)

In this example, we see children engaged in an attempt to make sense of a particular part of their experience. If we take science to be the progressive understanding of the biological and physical objects and events in the world around, then the activity certainly had a scientific focus. But it was scientific not just because of the subject matter, but because of the way in which the children engaged with it. They started from an idea which they thought explained the lowering of the water level in the tank. They realized that this was not the only possible explanation, and that it should be regarded as a 'might be' statement and not as a statement of 'what is'. So they put it to a test and made sure that they would eliminate some ambiguity in the result by using the control drops of water. They took note of the evidence, and those who had been convinced that the tank must be leaking changed their ideas.

This example illustrates that an important way in which learning in science comes about is through children using and testing their ideas as they attempt to make sense of the events and objects in the world around them. There are points that are worth particular note:

(1) The children had ideas to express about what they saw; they did not wait to be told about what was causing the water to 'disappear'.
(2) They changed their ideas in the light of the evidence gathered, not on the basis of what they or others thought or what they assumed.
(3) They tested their ideas by making a prediction (if the water is leaking out then the tank will be wet on the outside); but realizing that there could be another explanation for water not being seen outside the tank, they set up a test of the alternative hypothesis (that the leaked water could have dried up before they saw it).
(4) There was a social dimension to the work. The children were working as a group, discussing their work, exchanging ideas and challenging each other. It is conceivable that the control drops would not have been thought of by children working alone. The one child who thought about the need for the control drops introduced an idea that was taken up by others, but even the child who thought of it may have done so in response to the challenge from another child along the lines of, 'what if it dries up before we see it?'

The recognition that children do already have ideas about the things around them is emerging from a growing body of research into learning. It plays an important part in the view of learning in which learners themselves take a part in constructing meaning for themselves. This contrasts with the view of the child as having an empty mind into which knowledge is packed. When children's existing ideas are acknowledged, learning is regarded as change in these ideas brought about by testing them against evidence – in much the same way as scientists test their theories. The change may involve modification or rejection of initial ideas or the adoption of alternatives that fit the evidence better. Whichever it may be, the change is carried out by the child's own reasoning and the new ideas become his or her own.

The same view of learning was taken by the Science Working Group, which drew up the Secretary of State's proposals for the National Curriculum in science:

In their early experience of the world, pupils develop ideas which enable them to make sense of things that happen around them. They bring these informal ideas into the classroom and the aim of science education is to give pupils more explanatory power so that their ideas can become useful concepts.

For the child learning science, as for the scientist, the way understanding develops depends both on the existing ideas and on the processes by which those ideas are used and tested in new situations.

(NCC 1989, A7, paragraphs 6.2 and 6.3)

Reference has been made here and earlier to the comparison of children's learning with the work of scientists. There do appear to be many similarities. The scientist uses existing theories (generalizations) to attempt to make sense of new phenomena or to predict events. If evidence shows that the theory or predictions based on it do not fit reality, then some change may be made to the theory or an alternative tried. In this way, ideas and theories are modified so that they fit more of the available evidence, and thus become more powerful in helping understanding of a wider range of phenomena.

Implied in this view of science is that ideas and theories are always subject to modification as new evidence comes to hand. Thus accepted scientific theories are not regarded as fixed and immovable, but as the best way of understanding certain observations that have so far been found. Moreover, it should be noted that whether or not a theory is considered to fit evidence will depend in part on the way in which an experimental or theoretical test is carried out. The history of science provides many examples of theories being accepted when they should have been rejected, or vice versa, because of error in procedure and methods rather than the nature of the evidence.

Not everyone agrees that the nature of scientific thinking in children is basically the same as in adults and scientists (Kuhn, Amsel and O'Laughlin, 1988); the disagreement lies over the nature of the mechanism linking processes of thinking to the conceptual development rather than whether such a link exists.

THE PROCESS SKILL FOCUS OF STAR

The description of learning that we have given above argues that the way in which the existing ideas are linked to new events and are tested as possible explanations has a key role. Clearly, for the outcome it matters that notice is taken of the evidence and use is made of that evidence. These things involve skills and attitudes of reasoning and investigation, such as suggesting hypotheses or possible explanations that can be tested; planning and carrying out fair tests; observing carefully; interpreting findings; reviewing evidence and procedures critically and being willing to change ideas in the light of evidence. These skills are variously described as science processes, process skills or, simply, skills. Here the term 'process skill' is preferred since this avoids confusion with the sorts of specific and mechanical skills that are often implied when the term is used in other contexts. These process skills involve both mental and physical activity.

In Chapter 2, we take up the further identification and definition of the set of skills that formed the focus of the STAR project. Here our concern is to explain the reasons for this focus.

The description of learning in terms of changing ideas has important implications for the provision of opportunity for learning in classrooms. There are three aspects to be considered:

(1) the children's initial ideas;
(2) the processes of linking ideas and experience and testing one against the other;
(3) the nature of the experiences provided in the classroom.

The child's initial ideas must be explored and taken seriously if they are genuinely to form the starting point for learning. The teacher in the example at the beginning of this chapter was doing this by consciously asking the children to draw and talk about their ideas. The teacher then took each idea and worked out with the children a way of testing it (the example quoted only followed one of these tests – the other ideas led to further sequences of activities). It is important for teachers to have information about the ideas children commonly hold and about how they can explore and respond to the ideas of their own pupils.

The process skills are the means by which links are made between the ideas the children have based on their earlier experience and the new experiences which they encounter, and the means of testing these ideas to see if they help the understanding of the new experiences. As we have said, the ideas that emerge as an outcome of learning depend very much on how the linking and testing are carried out. If observation is superficial and takes no account of important detail, then unhelpful ideas may be linked (this happened when some children described wet blocks of wood that were sticking together as 'magnetic'). If some parts of the evidence is ignored, or if tests are carried out which are not 'fair' or lack necessary controls, then the emerging ideas will not be the ones which really fit the evidence. Ideas may persist which should be dismissed or useful ideas may be rejected because of reasoning which is flawed or not based on the evidence available.

In relation to (2), the learning experiences provided have to meet various criteria relating to the age, experience, interests and other skills of the children. They also have to be feasible in terms of the materials and equipment they require and the part which children can take in them with safety and confidence. They should also avoid cultural and gender bias (see NCC, 1989, para 7.10).

When any of these criteria is not met, there is lack of genuine learning opportunity. Experiences which, for example, are obscure or complicated by elaborate technology or require abstract ideas for their understanding, are unsuitable for young children because they are outside the reach of the children's existing ideas. They cannot be the basis for learning with understanding. Similarly, less complex things, but ones which do not appear relevant from the children's point of view (or the point of view of a section of the children), do not provide learning opportunities.

All three aspects are important for the development of good practice in primary science. Work has been seriously lacking with regard to (1) until the SPACE project began its work in 1987. Most activity in supporting science in the primary school has been devoted to (3), the provision of classroom activities and a vast choice of programmes and schemes now exists. Some of the curriculum materials developed have discussed and supported the use of process skills in general terms rather than being specifically designed to encourage the development of these skills. On the other hand, work which has a specific process focus has comprised exercises in skill development out of the context of children's investigation of things around them. Thus, perhaps surprisingly, the focus on (2) has been neglected.

The STAR project saw it as important to address the development of children's process skills for the following reasons:

- these skills play a key role in the learning of science;
- the neglect of attention to the development, as opposed to the occasional use, of these skills in children through normal classroom activities;
- the recognition that teachers needed help if they were to give more attention to the development of children's process skills.

The project did not see the development of these skills as either the means to the end of concept development, nor an end in itself. Because concepts are being constantly developed, not just in the years of formal education, but throughout life, there is a need for continued development of the process skills to the levels where they can further the development of more abstract and powerful ideas.

Thus the process skill focus was chosen for STAR because of the value of these skills in the process of understanding and the construction of ideas and concepts, not because they were considered to be more important than conceptual development. The project's aim was to maintain this focus while

- considering the process skills in the context of normal science activities;
- working within what was feasible within the regular classroom with all its distractions and multiple demand on teachers
- accepting and building upon teachers' own starting points in the understanding of process skills and of how to assist their development in children.

CLASSROOM OBSERVATION AND THE ASSESSMENT OF PUPILS

The process of scientific thinking described earlier clearly places considerable responsibility on the teacher. As was seen in the chapter's opening episode, the teacher's role is not simply that of a facilitator whose task it is to provide a suitable environment in which children are presented with new opportunities for learning. In the classroom, teachers provide information, make suggestions, and initiate and respond to questions, thereby helping children make sense of new experiences. In a busy primary classroom with upwards of twenty-four children, a teacher might engage in a dozen such conversations with different pupils in the course of a minute. A number of studies, besides the initial one carried out by Rowe (1974), have shown that when questioning pupils the average length of time between the teacher's question and either the pupil's reply or a further question or prompt from the teacher is often less than three seconds (Tobin, 1984). On the basis of these short encounters, teachers have to arrive at judgements about the stage that the children's thinking has reached. Clearly if the teacher's hypothesis as to what is going on in the pupil's mind is false, then any subsequent interventions by the teacher are likely to be unhelpful to the pupil.

Recently, there have been a number of studies which have attempted to help the teacher carry through this diagnostic role. At secondary level, for example, researchers have studied concept formation in secondary mathematics and science (Hart, 1981). This work highlights the importance of the process of taking pupils back over the various steps in the task to see where they went wrong as a means of discovering where the 'learner is at'. Similar strategies involving a post-task interview of this kind have been used by Bennett *et al.* (1984) at primary level to establish the degree of mis-match between the tasks set by teachers and the capacity of the pupils to cope with the task with minimal support from the teacher.

However, there are grave, practical problems with this suggestion. While most teachers will readily acknowledge that such an approach can provide helpful information about a pupil's process of thinking, post-task interviews are very time consuming. The classroom teacher, therefore, has to compromise and reserve this approach for cases where there are serious learning problems. On most occasions, teachers will first try to arrive at an understanding of 'where the pupil is at' by listening and watching the pupil at work. A pupil's actions can often provide clues to the way he or she is thinking and can be used by the teacher to lessen the risk of incorrect diagnosis.

There are, however, problems when teachers attempt to interpret observations for this purpose. First an observer will often carry with them preconceived notions concerning the motives which lie behind another person's actions. This can lead the observer to develop expectations that cause subsequent behaviours to be interpreted within this preconceived framework. For example in some cultures it is a mark of disrespect to an adult if a child does not direct his gaze towards the ground when being admonished. In our culture, a teacher might regard a child who did not maintain eye contact with the teacher when being told off as 'shifty' and perhaps interpret future behaviour as 'sly' or dishonest.

A second difficulty when attempting to make sense of our observations concerns a tendency for individuals, when presented with evidence of failure, to attribute reasons for such failure to circumstances that lie beyond the control of the individual. In this way, we are able to absolve ourselves from any responsibility for the failure. Teachers are continually placed in such situations during observation of pupils. They may set children to work together in groups and observe that some children are not participating fully in the activity. They may observe some children fooling around or not paying attention when addressing the whole class. In such circumstances, teachers will be likely to attribute the cause of these observed events either to the background of pupils, some feature of the classroom environment, or to the limited availability of resources. In one study, for example, where over 200 teachers were confronted with the pupils' failure to respond to teachers' 'higher-order' questions, not one individual considered that one possible cause might be the way in which the question had been asked. Most teachers suggested that either the children were not capable, at this particular age, of engaging in such a cognitive activity, or that their particular home background was not one which encouraged the children to engage in thinking skills of this kind (Beckman, 1976).

In the STAR project there were several examples of similar causal attributions leading to a possible wrong diagnosis. Pupils in one class were asked to solve a practical problem by working collaboratively in a group. The pupils failed to come up with a plausible solution and the teacher concluded that this was because at the age of seven, they were not capable of working independently from the teacher. She decided, therefore, that tasks of this kind needed to be done under the close direction of the teacher. Her informal observations of the children supported this view because she tended to highlight only those pupil exchanges which indicated lack of co-operation.

The third difficulty encountered by a class teacher when attempting to diagnose pupils' learning through observation concerns the selective nature of such an activity. In teaching, as with other activities, what we register as having occurred is sometimes at variance with what actually happened. One dramatic illustration of this was recorded by Galton (1988) where until informed by other teachers of his behaviour, he could not recall having raised his voiced or banged a table. Other examples have been provided by Elliott (1976). There, in the Ford Teaching Project, teachers were unaware of the extent to which they had led the discussion during the introduction to a discovery style lesson until they listened to a tape recording. These perception gaps occur because our actions are governed not only by the way we think, but by the way we feel. We sometimes have uncomfortable feelings which we wish to suppress and unconsciously ignore those behaviours which are a response to such feelings. In a discovery style lesson, for example, asking pupils questions which call for a range of speculative answers on the part of the pupils can pose a threat to our self-image as teachers. To the public, the teacher is someone who knows the answers. Teaching is popularly associated with telling. Allowing pupils to offer answers to questions to which we ourselves may not know the answers therefore runs contrary to the popular conception of 'a good teacher'. Even though, intellectually, we may reject this, our unconscious need for parental approval may lead us to behave in ways that limit pupils' freedom to answer the questions in ways they would like. In one example of a lesson observed during the ORACLE project (Galton *et al.*, 1980), a teacher introduced the topic of pollution and children were invited to think about ways in which the environment could be affected. The teacher, however, had in the back of his mind the possibility of an experiment where the children could investigate the degree of pollution in samples of water. The video recording of the lesson showed clearly that whenever a pupil mentioned water, for example, talking about pollution in the sea, the teacher smiled and wrote down the pupil's answer on the board in larger writing than when another pupil offered an example of pollution on land. Asked about the lesson afterwards the pupils said it was satisfactory, once they knew the teacher wanted them 'to do water'.

The above discussion is not intended to present a case against the use of classroom observation as an important means of gaining clues about pupils' thinking. The aim is to sound a note of caution against the claims made by some writers such as Spooner (1980) that as teachers gain experience, they become better observers and are able to judge and interpret their pupils' behaviour without training or support from colleagues. It would be of less concern to challenge such views if the judgements of teachers were not so important in determining the future of their pupils. In the ORACLE transfer studies, for example, there were few cases where pupils overturned the predictions of their primary teachers during their time in the secondary school (Delamont and Galton, 1986).

METHODS OF CLASSROOM OBSERVATION

In seeking to overcome the difficulties associated with teacher judgements, researchers have developed a number of procedures based upon classroom observation. It is not being suggested that, when teachers use these observation techniques, it is necessary to go to the same lengths as researchers who require a very high degree of correspondence between what is recorded and what actually takes place. Inevitably, observation by a class teacher must be a compromise between what is practical and what is desirable. In arriving at this compromise, however, teachers need to be aware of the principles behind the different approaches to classroom observation, and the strengths and weaknesses of the respective methods. Given the earlier discussion, for example, a teacher who wished to base his or her judgements of pupil's motivation on personal informal observations would do well to look for other kinds of evidence to support conclusions about non-conforming pupils.

Broadly speaking, two methods of observation have been developed for use in classrooms. The first method, at different times called interaction analysis, systematic observation or structured observation, seeks to define each particular behaviour of interest in an unambiguous way so that different observers viewing the same events will record them in the same manner. Structured observation requires an observer to code each behaviour event in such a way that a permanent record of it is obtained. Sometimes, the event itself is also captured permanently when what takes place during the lesson is recorded on video or audio tape. Most structured observation systems, however, require the observer to be present in the classroom and to code events as they happen. Structured observation was the method used in the STAR project and the reasons for making this choice will be considered in Chapter 3.

The alternative approach to classroom observation is often known as 'participant observation'. Unlike structured observation where the observer attempts to remain outside the action (the fly on the wall approach), in participant observation the observer takes an active role in the proceedings. The situation is best defined by Sara Delamont as follows:

The particular model presented here is drawn from the ideas of a group of authors, some sociologists and some social psychologists, who call themselves symbolic interactionists. This sounds formidable, but it is not difficult to understand because it embodies an approach to the study of human life very close to the way we run our ordinary lives. If you imagine yourself taking a new job in a strange milieu – say as a ward orderly in a large hospital – think how you would learn the job. Probably you would watch other orderlies, ask them about what you should be doing, and you would observe how other people expected you to behave. The other orderlies, the nurses and doctors, and possibly the patients would all give you advice, warnings and direct instructions. If you were wise you would gather as much information as you could and use it to become a good orderly. At first it would feel strange – like acting on stage – but gradually you would become a ward orderly for long periods of time. Every time we enter a new social situation – a job, a school, a household or a relationship – we learn how to behave by watching and asking and listening.

At its simplest, being a symbolic interactionist means doing research by observation and participation and not by testing, measuring and experimenting. Of course, anyone could do research this way. It is often called participant observation because the observer talks to, and participates in activities with, the people she is studying. Anthropologists have always worked like this when studying exotic tribes.

(Delamont, 1976 p. 36)

Behind this approach lies a conviction that actions only have meaning as a result of the shared understandings that individuals have about events in which they played a part. Thus one important characteristic of the participant observation approach is the use of triangulation procedures, whereby the same event is interpreted through the eyes of different participants. In the Ford Teaching Project, referred to earlier, the views of the teacher, the pupils and the researcher about the same lesson were compared (Elliott, 1976). This is called 'between observer triangulation'. As an alternative, in Delamont's (1976) study of a Scottish girls' school, friendship patterns between pupils were observed during lessons, measured from sociograms and deduced from the choices that pupils made when invited to take tea with Delamont, in groups of three, outside school. This is termed 'between methods triangulation'.

Consideration of the debate that has taken place about the advantages and disadvantages of these two methods of observation is beyond the scope of this book. In general, it is fair to say that nowadays the two methods are seen as complementing each other rather than alternative approaches (Galton and Delamont, 1985). Structured observation is often criticized because it simply provides frequency counts of events. As such the descriptions of classroom events lack colour. Participant accounts of classrooms, on the other hand, often yield vivid descriptions of what it is like to be a teacher or a pupil, but it is difficult to check the accuracy of these descriptions, nor do we know if they are generalizable beyond the particular classroom where the events took place. A full discussion of these problems of reliability and validity can be found in Croll (1986) and Burgess (1985).

CLASSROOM OBSERVATION AND THE TEACHER

Some structured observation systems used in research are extremely complicated. For example, in the research project, Curriculum Provision in Small Primary Schools (PRISMS), the observation schedule consisted of over 100 categories, some of which the observers had to code every five seconds. To operate this system reliably required at least two weeks training (Galton and Patrick, 1990). Other structured observation systems such as Flanders Interaction Analysis System (Flanders, 1970) have only ten categories, and can be learned with only half a day's training. Systems like that of Flanders, however, will only describe very broad categories of behaviour. For example, in Flanders there is a category, 'teachers ask questions' but in studying science processes in the classroom, we wish to know something about the nature of these questions, whether they are concerned to elicit information or require pupils to make inferences, etc. The Flanders system would therefore be unsuitable. In general, the easier the system is to use, the less justice it does to the complexity of events in the classroom.

A teacher left to his or her own devices will, however, generally only be able to observe broad categories of behaviour. Alternatively, the teacher could, when seeking more precise information about particular science processes, concentrate on one or two categories on any one occasion, for example, on the extent to which pupils plan experiments during one lesson and on the ways in which pupils hypothesize during the next. The teacher alone in the classroom may also choose to concentrate on a group of pupils rather than observe the whole class, particularly in cases where other information has led the teacher to make a negative assessment about certain pupils' aptitudes. A teacher could also make a tape recording of children during a lesson and subsequently analyse this in terms of a set of determined categories. This latter strategy should, however, be used sparingly, as most researchers agree that one hour of audio tape requires a week to analyse.

Whenever possible it is a considerable benefit to have either an outside observer or a colleague to work alongside the teacher. Those fortunate enough to work near a University Department or a College of Education can ask staff in these institutions to act as consultants and, under certain conditions, it is possible for student teachers to act as observers, as in the IT-INSET approach (Everton and Impey, 1989).

The most readily available resource, however, is a colleague. Schools who value the part that observation can play in bringing about improvements in teaching and learning, can usually find ways whereby two teachers can work together with one of the pair acting as an observer. Sometimes the headteacher will volunteer to take one of the classes. At other times, another teacher with the help of parents, could take two classes or register groups thus freeing a colleague to act as an observer elsewhere. Sometimes, year group assemblies can free other teachers, while in some schools there are specialists for PE and music who can provide space in the time-table for class teachers to observe. The advent of standard assessment tasks within the National Curriculum should greatly increase the need for teachers within schools to work together in these ways.

In participant observation, in addition to the views of colleagues or outside observers, it will usually be necessary to elicit the opinions of pupils. This can be a problem for the class teacher because pupils will often tend to report what they think the teacher wishes to hear, rather than what they themselves feel or think. There are, however, a number of important 'projective techniques' for eliciting pupils' viewpoints. One such technique developed by Cavendish (1988), involves the use of cartoon pictures or drawings of different teaching situations. Cavendish invited, for example, children to write down what they thought was happening in a cartoon picture in which pupils were sitting around a table doing a mathematics worksheet. The same technique has been used by Cowell (1990), a teacher-observer who took part in the STAR project, to discover pupils' views on science and science teaching. Similar approaches, using actual photographs of lessons, have been used at secondary level by Walker and Wiedel (1985) and in the reception class of an infant school by Barrett (1986).

Experience suggests that, initially, teachers find it easier to begin with structured observation systems rather than engage in participant approaches. As Delamont has remarked, one of the difficulties of participant observation is that it tends to focus on the unusual, and observers find it difficult to describe the regular, routine, matter-of-fact events which make up a considerable part of classroom life. Participant accounts are likely to focus on incidents where there is loss of control or where pupils fool around and are not paying attention, rather than on periods where nothing dramatic takes place and pupils are working conscientiously. In cases of disruption, it is likely to be less stressful for a teacher to be told by an observer colleague that one per cent of all observations involved misbehaviour, rather than be informed that while you, the teacher, were helping Anne and Tim, Jason was punching Debbie and that she retaliated by pulling his hair. It requires considerable social skill for a teacher to act as an observer in such situations and not to distort the account through fear of embarrassing a colleague, nor to imply ineffective classroom management on the part of the teacher. It is sometimes thought that participant observation is a soft option. This discussion should have served to indicate that both types of observation require special skills and a degree of training, a point reinforced by researchers (Delamont and Galton, 1986).

THE USE OF SPOC AS A RESEARCH INSTRUMENT

As discussed earlier in the chapter, if the teacher is to be helpful to pupils in their development of science process skills, then he or she must constantly attempt to assess what is going on in the pupil's mind. This is a difficult task since the teacher cannot assess a pupil's thinking by collecting evidence of thought directly. When we see a child staring into space we do not know if the child is thinking about the task or about other matters, nor do we know what these thoughts are about. We are reduced, therefore, to collecting evidence from the products of children's thinking. In the past, these products have generally been taken to be written work, with teachers basing their assessment of the children's conceptual development on suppositions made from the marking and subsequent interpretation of the writing in exercise books and folder work; but the things children say and do are also products of their thinking and an equally admissable source of evidence.

In order that children can display their level of thinking, the opportunity to do so must be provided by the teacher. It may be that the task content or context, or the composition of the groups of pupils working together, affects the behaviour and interactions of the children. The teacher must bear these factors in mind when making assessments of their pupils. One way of providing the maximum opportunity for children to display particular skills is to set a specially-designed practical task accompanied by in-depth questioning, a method utilized by the STAR project and discussed fully in a subsequent book in this series by Russell and Harlen (1990). This method requires one assessor for one child and would, of course, be very time consuming if every child in a class was to be assessed in this way. An alternative and more feasible method of collecting evidence for assessing a majority of the pupils, is for the teachers to carry out observation during normal classroom activities. The questions children raise with each other and the ideas they put forward, as illustrated by the example at the beginning of this chapter, can provide insights into the process skills children use. Observation does not necessarily have to be of individual children, but can be directed at a group of several children working together. The information collected would serve to indicate whether the activity provided an opportunity for the group of pupils to display certain skills and, if so, which children made use of this opportunity and which did not. Knowing that an individual child did not make use of such opportunities, while other children did, is useful assessment material for the teacher, who can then investigate in more depth, on a one-to-one basis, whether the particular child actually lacks the skill, or was unable to project him or herself in the group setting in which he or she was placed.

One of the aims of the STAR project was to develop an instrument suitable for carrying out this kind of observation during science lessons. This development drew on previous in-service experience (Harlen, 1985) and on the ORACLE research study (Galton *et al.*, 1980). In the STAR project, the main purpose was to gather information about pupils' use of the eight science process skills which had earlier been identified by Harlen (1985) and the observation instrument subsequently developed became known as the Science Process Observation Categories (SPOC). The observation instrument was required to serve two functions: first, to act as a research tool to gather information about the classroom situation while the interaction was taking place; and, second, to act as a basis from which teachers could develop an instrument for their own use within their own and their colleagues' classrooms. These two functions are rather different. From necessity, the research version was essentially a fuller and more complicated instrument. It is described fully in Chapter 4. When used by teachers, it had to be modified so that the teacher could code pupil interactions while teaching in their own classroom. Several versions were developed and tried out by the STAR teachers and are described in Chapter 6.

Initially, the SPOC observation instrument was designed for research purposes only. During the first year of the STAR project, information was gathered for baseline data, to describe existing classroom practice during the teaching of primary science. Information concerning the extent of pupil interactions taking place in the classroom, and how much intervention by the teacher was involved in these interactions, was recorded. This baseline data was fed back to the participating teachers at the end of the first year of the project, when they attended a conference. The purpose of this exercise was to encourage teachers to reflect on how closely their own classrooms matched the general patterns of data, and to consider how they might explore different strategies for developing the science process skills which the observations showed were used infrequently by their pupils. For example, if frequent interaction about scientific observations and planning were observed, but infrequent interaction about critical reflection or hypothesizing, then teachers were challenged to think about how to encourage the little-used process skills and to improve the quality of the frequently-used skills.

During the second year of the project, teachers practised and evaluated the various strategies for improving the frequency and quality of two or three process skills of their choice. Observation of children continued, but instead of using the information gathered solely for research purposes, the observers and teachers discussed the results at the end of each session. The feedback provided helped the teachers to evaluate the lesson and to plan the way forward for the next science session. It was important that the observer simply presented the results of the observation, and not opinions concerning the effectiveness of the interactions, so that the evaluation of the lesson was made by the teacher, although with the advantage of having the help of an extra pair of eyes and ears inside the classroom.

The third year of the project saw the continuation of some observation by researchers, but this was now supplemented by teacher observation. Teachers worked with a colleague, observing in the classroom of the colleague as well as in their own room or base area. The form of the observation instrument thus changed as now it had to be easy, and suitable for use while the teacher-observer was also engaged in teaching. Differences in teaching styles had to be considered when establishing a successful strategy for observation. One teacher taught science by means of group work, another engaged in team teaching; and the strategy adopted for the management of the classroom greatly affected the time and opportunity for observation of each other within the classroom.

The adaptation of SPOC for teacher use was done with varying degrees of success. Some teachers declared the need for more information than merely the process skills – the grouping of children, task content, resources used, etc. Indeed, one group of teachers eventually included nearly all of the categories listed on the original research instrument. Another group preferred to take field notes during the lesson and to transfer the information to a sheet of category headings afterwards. Another group wished to have more detailed information about the science process skills than the global terms offered in SPOC, for example, controlling of variables and making a fair test. A description of the various methods used is presented in Chapter 6.

The STAR project brought together teachers from four local education authorities. The teachers shared each others' experiences and observation techniques, and this sharing led to teachers reflecting on their own situations to see if they could effect further improvement by adapting and developing another teacher's strategies. This book is about sharing – sharing the experiences of the STAR research team, and sharing the experiences of the participating STAR teachers.

2

Process Skills in Action

In Chapter 1 we have considered the role of process skills in learning, and argued that it is important to know about the extent of children's experience of these skills in order to further their learning. Here we take up two related questions. First, which process skills are thought to be important and how should they be described? Second, what is the nature of these skills, how can they be identified in action, and what are the observable indicators that children are using them?

RATIONALE FOR THE STAR LIST OF PROCESS SKILLS

The STAR project's view of learning in science, as indicated in Chapter 1, is that it is a process of developing ideas, skills and attitudes which help in making sense of the world around. Ideas are progressively developed by being tested against evidence and, as the expanding experience of children makes new evidence available, so ideas are modified to become more widely applicable.

This overall description is rather too general to be useful for guiding teaching and learning, and a more analytical approach is necessary. Specific skills, though rarely used in isolation, can nevertheless be identified as parts of the whole called 'investigation' or 'exploration' or 'making sense of the world'. The analytical approach is not unfamiliar in science projects, and is seen in the broad aims of Science 5/13. The project's overall purpose of 'Developing an enquiring mind and a scientific approach to problems' was broken down into:

- developing interests, attitudes and aesthetic awareness;
- observing, exploring and ordering observations;
- developing basis concepts and logical thinking;
- posing questions and devising experiments or investigations to answer them;
- acquiring knowledge and learning skills;
- communicating;
- appreciating patterns and relationships;
- interpreting findings critically.

(Ennever and Harlen, 1972)

Another familiar list is found in the first five categories of the APU framework. Categories of skills which together constituted 'Performing investigations' were described as:

- use of symbolic representation;
- use of apparatus and measuring instruments;
- observation;
- interpretation and application;
- planning investigations.

The APU used the same framework of skill categories for its work at both primary and secondary levels. The DES also saw no difference between primary and secondary phases when, in *Science 5–16: A Statement of Policy*, it stated that pupils at all stages should be given appropriate opportunities to:

- make observations;
- select observations relevant to their investigations for further study;
- seek and identify patterns and relate these to patterns perceived earlier;
- suggest and evaluate explanations of the patterns;
- design and carry out experiments, including appropriate forms of measurement, to test suggested explanations for the patterns of observations;
- communicate (verbally, mathematically and graphically) and interpret written and other material;
- handle equipment safely and effectively;
- use knowledge in conducting investigations;
- bring their knowledge to bear in attempting to solve technological problems.

(DES, 1985, pp. 3–4)

While being aware of and sharing much of the philosophy behind these lists, the STAR set of process skills was not derived from them, but from consideration of the nature of science activities and of what skills it was useful for teachers to identify as separate foci for children's development, and hence for assessment and review.

There is no one 'model' for the sequence of events within science investigations in school, any more than there is an agreed model for scientific investigations at any level. Some activities start from observations of certain objects or phenomena, about which questions are raised. Questions which can be investigated then lead to the planning of further actions – for 'fair tests', perhaps, which may supply the answers. During the course of these tests and enquiries, further observations will be made, possibly involving measurement. Records may be made and there will be some interpretation of what is found. The series of linked activities could end up with an attempt to propose hypotheses, that is, suggested explanations for what was found. This is likely to happen in the course of discussion which encourages the critical review of evidence and of the procedures used for collecting it.

An example of such a series of events might arise from children observing the phenomenon of chromatography, or the rise of water by capillary action up a strip of absorbent paper. While observing the latter, one group of ten year olds posed questions about the rise of the water up the paper which included:

Will it go on going up for ever?
Will it go faster with thicker paper?
Does the same happen if there's something in the water?
Can we try it with hot water?
Is there something special about this paper?

It was not difficult for the children to work out plans for an investigation to find the answers to each of these questions. They worked out ways to compare the effect of the thickness of the paper, making sure to keep the other dimensions and the type of paper the same. They also tried different types of paper. Here they became interested in whether the speed with which the water rose was related to the eventual height it reached, and some ingenious ways of measuring speed were tried. The most satisfactory was to mark parallel horizontal lines on the paper and note the time when the water reached each one. The question was also asked, 'Why does it do it?' The teacher did not ignore this question but turned it into a reason for the other investigations, replying that, 'If we find out these other things then that might help you to work out why it happens'.

On the other hand, sometimes activities start from a conjecture (hypothesis) about why certain observed happenings are taking place. There may be more than one feasible explanation, and there is a need to devise investigations to test each one. These tests involve planning, ensuring procedures for 'fairness' in the tests, observing, comparing and possibly measuring changes which take place, interpreting and reviewing what is found in terms of the competing explanations. This kind of sequence of events took place when, in a topic on movement, children rolled cylindrical cans with different contents down a slope. There was a distinct difference in the speed with which the cans started rolling and the distance they eventually reached. The children had immediate reasons for this. Some thought that the very small differences in the sizes of the can could explain the differences in movement. Others focused on the different masses, others on the different constitution of the contents made obvious by shaking the cans. These hypotheses were tested by investigations which the children planned. They used other containers so that they could control their size and contents, and were necessarily involved in some careful measurements of mass, volume and dimensions of a cylinder in the process.

Again, the starting point can be a problem of some kind. Which material to choose for a certain purpose is a common stimulus that leads to planning and carrying through fair tests based on what are thought to be important variables. Many examples of these 'which is best for . . .?' activities could be given. Some of the activities in which teachers and children were involved in testing scraps of fabric to find 'which would be best for keeping us dry' are indicated in the summary in Figure 2.1. It is easy to see that measurement, observation, recording, interpreting findings and critically reviewing are represented there.

Other problems which are useful starting points for science activities are

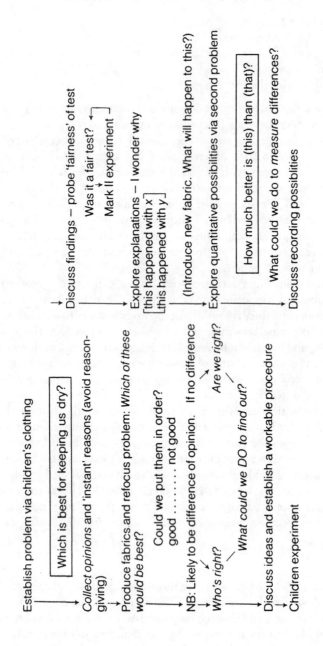

Figure 2.1   *The place of process skills in a science activity on the testing of fabrics (Harlen and Jelly, 1989.)*

challenges about how to make something happen. How to make a sunflower seed grow into a really tall plant; how to build the strongest bridge from paper; how to make two bulbs light up equally strongly from one battery, etc. In each case the solving of the problem requires some understanding of the relationships and properties of materials involved. This understanding will come through investigation based on questions raised through trying out initial ideas.

These are just examples of what is an endless variety of activities. What they have in common is that there is potential in all of them for children:

    to observe
    to raise investigable questions
    to hypothesize
    to plan
    to measure
    to interpret data
    to record and communicate
    to reflect critically.

The potential for every one of these skills to be used may not be realized in each activity, for it will depend on the age of the children concerned and what they see as the purpose of the activity at the time. Thus we are not expecting every skill to be represented in every activity, but the role that each skill can have means that it is a relevant dimension of science activities.

There are naturally very many ways of expressing these skills; the different words used is sometimes a cause of confusion. This is part of the reason why it is important to agree on an operational definition, that is, one that indicates what it means for children to be carrying out the skill, whatever title is given to it.

The skills involved in investigation have now been spelled out in the National Curriculum, which was developed between 1987 and 1988. It is interesting to compare these skills with the STAR list which was devised in early 1986, long before work began on defining the science curriculum. The relevant part of the National Curriculum for Science is Attainment Target 1 'Exploration of Science' (DES, 1989). Figure 2.2 compares the criteria which define Level 2 (which it is expected will be reached by the majority of seven year olds), and those for Level 4 (which the majority of eleven year olds are expected to reach) with the STAR list of skills.

THE VALUE OF OBSERVING PROCESS SKILLS IN ACTION

The key role of process skills in learning means that understanding (as opposed to rote memorization) depends on children obtaining and using evidence for themselves, and carrying out the physical and mental skills which this implies. Unlike products of learning activities which, once created, remain in existence, the processes in which skills are used take place in real time. This presents a challenge for gathering information about process skills, for whatever purpose.

One solution is to observe events while they are happening, when direct, if

National Curriculum Level 2	STAR	National Curriculum Level 4
Identify simple differences	Observation	
List and collate observations		
Ask questions and suggest ideas of the 'how', 'why', and 'what will happen if' variety	Raising investigable questions	Raise questions in a form which can be investigated
	Hypothesizing	Formulate testable hypotheses
	Planning	Construct 'fair tests'
		Plan an investigation where the plan indicates that the relevant variables have been identified and others controlled.
Use standard and non-standard measures	Measuring	Select and use a range of measuring instruments, as appropriate, to quantify observations of physical quantities.
Record findings in charts, drawings and other appropriate forms	Recording and communicating	Follow written instructions and diagrammatic representations
		Record results by appropriate means such as the construction of simple tables, bar charts, line graphs
		Describe investigations in the form of ordered prose, using limited technical vocabulary
	Interpreting data	Draw conclusions from experimental results
	Reflecting critically	

Figure 2.2 *A comparison of STAR process skills with the National Curriculum Attainment Target 1, Levels 2 and 4.*

transitory, evidence is obtained. Another solution is to devise tasks in which certain outcomes can only be reached by the use of process skills, so that it can be assumed that the product is evidence of the use of the process skills. This approach has been adopted in many cases for the purpose of assessment. For instance, questions in the Walled Garden assessment (Schilling *et al.*, 1990) were devised with the intention that certain of the STAR process skills had to be used. Although these written tasks necessarily have the disadvantage of involving other abilities (particularly reading and writing) as well as the science process skills, they have the advantage of convenience for the purpose of pupil assessment. Evidence of the same kind can also be found from children's regular work providing the need to use process skills is part of that work.

In this book, we are concerned not only with gathering information for assessing children's performance of the process skills, but also for finding out how much opportunity they have of employing and developing these skills in their normal work. Such information has an on-going function in teaching. It could be argued that there is little point in assessing what children can do if they have no opportunity to learn how to do it, and thus that opportunity should be ascertained before any assessment is worthwhile. However, it is also argued that the interpretation of assessment raises questions about the extent of children's opportunities which may not otherwise be posed. A low level of performance of a child or group should be interpreted in the light of information about relevant learning experiences, and the frequency and nature of those experiences. Thus such information has a key role in the interpretation and formative use of assessment.

As we have said, in order to make observations about whether or not a process skill is being used, there must be some shared understanding about what is to be taken as evidence of use. This is particularly necessary because of the differences in understanding which exist about the meaning of 'interpreting data', 'raising questions' and even 'hypothesizing'. It is helpful, therefore, to have some descriptions in terms of what children do. Such statements of indicators (Harlen, 1985, p. 111) were developed for the STAR process skills and the rest of this chapter is devoted to presenting and discussing them.

INDICATORS OF PROCESS SKILLS

In Chapter 1 the role of process skills in learning with understanding, that is, developing ideas from one's own experience and thinking, was described, and the arguments for the process skill focus of the STAR project were based on it. Because of the close connection between concept development and the use of process skills, it was argued that it was necessary to foster consciously the development of these skills. Only if they develop in sophistication can they continue to have a role in learning as experience expands and concepts become progressively more abstract and generalized.

There is, however, a two-way inter-relationship between process skills and concepts. Conceptual learning depends on the use of process skills, but at the same time the use of process skills is influenced by existing concepts about the subject matter under investigation. In making an observation, planning an investigation, giving an account or contributing to a group discussion, there has to be some content, for each has to be about something. What the 'something' is makes a considerable difference to the performance. For example, we make more relevant and detailed observations of something familiar than of something unfamiliar; we are more likely to plan a fair test if we know what can affect the result than if we do not; we can contribute more effectively to a group discussion if we feel comfortable with the topic being discussed than otherwise.

Two things follow from this which are relevant to the discussion below. First is that when a child is observed performing a certain level of skill in an investigation of X, it does not follow that the same level of skill will be shown in an investigation of Y. The point becomes obvious if we suggest that X is finding the relationship between how a paper aeroplane flies and the shape of its wings, and Y is the relationship between the concentration of a solution and its osmotic pressure. What we learn from seeing a child perform a skill is that the child is capable of using the skill at a particular level given certain circumstances. The conceptual demand of the subject matter has a considerable influence on the degree to which children are able to use skills shown in one context, and those shown in another quite different one.

The second point is that preconceived ideas and prior knowledge can interfere with children's willingness to gather and use evidence. If they feel that they 'know' the answer, then, whether they do or not, this will tend to 'short-circuit' investigation. For all of us, recall is quicker than working things out, so if we suppose we already have the answer, we will try this first. Over-familiarity of subject matter may therefore be as misleading as total unfamiliarity as far as indicating children's use of process skills is concerned.

In all cases, then, the interpretation of the observation of children's use of process skills should be within the context of the opportunities provided by an activity. We should be cautious of generalizing widely from this, but rather we should use the information to show what a child can do given the opportunity. The challenge is for us to help the child transfer skills from one context to another.

Observation

Observation is a wide term used in relation to all areas of the curriculum. It therefore requires careful definition in the context of science in order to avoid the pitfall of describing any reaction of a child to the environment as evidence of observation. In particular, we are not concerned merely with 'seeing', but with using all of the senses, where it is appropriate and safe to do so. Thus noting the different smells of threads of wool, cotton and synthetic fibre when carefully ignited, would be an instance of a relevant scientific observation in seeking differences in the burning of these materials.

Attention to detail is another feature of observation skill and one in which development can be seen; noticing only gross features develops into noticing details. 'Noticing' here is, of course, something which has to be inferred from what children do as a result of observation, since we cannot have direct access to their sense perception. What children say about what they see, smell, hear, or feel is an important source of evidence of their observation. This underlines the value of classroom discussion. Evidence also comes from written work, drawings, models and opportunities to translate observations into role play or drama. An example of the latter occurred when children were trying to reproduce, as effects for a play, the sound of a thunderstorm. Close and critical listening was necessary to arrive at what they wanted.

The relevance of the detail noticed to the problem in hand is a dimension of development of the skill of observation. It is here that the concept dependence of this skill is most easily detected. For example, the non-relevance of the colour of the plastic cover of a wire to whether it will help to light up a bulb is a matter of experience and knowledge. So this detail would be irrelevant to someone with this knowledge but not necessarily for someone without it.

In the context of classroom activities, investigations which involve comparing things provide opportunities for children to show the development in observation skill. Being able to identify differences between objects or events which are similar, or changes in the same thing as a result of taking some action, is an important part of many investigations. Even more significant is being able to identify similarities between events or objects which are different from each other. This involves making some links between the things in question, a process which plays a part in the widening of concepts, and is thus an important aspect of how observation helps the development of children's understanding.

In summary, then, the indicators of a child using observation, can be expressed as the following behaviours:

- notices gross features of a phenomenon or object;
- notices details of a phenomenon or object;
- focuses on observations relevant to the problem in hand;
- notices two similarities between different objects or events;
- notices two differences between similar objects or events.

Raising Questions

Asking investigable questions is essential to scientific investigation of any kind. A precursor for children is asking all kinds of question – investigable, philosophical, ones requiring information, names and conventions. Children do this quite naturally, but they can be easily discouraged, sometimes unintentionally, from doing so. An early stage in asking questions which leads to scientific investigation is thus to ask questions of any kind, to show curiosity about the things around. Gradually, as a result of trying to find answers to questions of different kinds, children become able to distinguish between questions which can be answered by investigation, e.g. 'Which of these kites will fly highest?', from those which cannot be answered in this way because they are matters of aesthetic judgement, e.g. 'Which kite is more attractive?', or require a different kind of debate, e.g. 'Why do people like flying kites?'.

The development of young children's scientific thinking is helped by asking a particular kind of question, the question which can be answered by the child's own enquiry. This is therefore the main focus of attention here and does not deny the value of children asking other kinds of questions. Often children's questions are expressed in terms of 'how' or 'why', and do not seem investigable, e.g. 'Why do woodlice curl up?' While this is not the place to go into how teachers can handle children's questions (e.g. Harlen, 1985, and Jelly, 1985), it is generally possible to respond in a way which turns such a question into an investigable one, by asking the child, for example, 'Are you sure that all woodlice do curl up?' or 'Why do you think it might be?' The child's question then becomes turned into, 'Do all kinds of woodlice curl up?', or 'Do woodlice curl up when . . .?' (whatever the child's suggestion had been).

Gradually, children begin to pick up this way of questioning. Development of the skill shows in the ability to express questions in more precise terms such that the information required is clear and, eventually, such that the kind of investigation required to obtain it is also specified. A question such as, 'Does sugar dissolve better in tea when it is stirred?', is not strictly in investigable form (what does 'better' mean – that more will dissolve, that it will dissolve faster, or that in some way the disappearance is more complete?). When expressed as 'Does sugar dissolve more quickly in tea when it is stirred?', it is investigable. A further step is to express it as, 'Does sugar dissolve more quickly in stirred tea than in tea which is not stirred?', because not only is the variable to be observed (the speed of dissolving) specified, but the variable to be changed (the stirring) is made explicit. The variable whose effect is to be observed (here the stirring) is called the independent variable, because it can be changed independently of anything else. The variable which may change as a result (in this case the speed of dissolving), is called the dependent variable because it is the result of changing something else on which it is dependent.

These points about how children show the ability to raise investigable questions can be summarized in the following indicators:

- raises more than one question (any kind);
- raises at least one question which is potentially investigable although the dependent variable may not be specified;
- expresses at least one question in investigable form;
- distinguishes when requested between a question which can be answered by investigation and other types;
- can reformulate a potentially investigable but vague question into one in which the independent and dependent variables are identified.

Hypothesizing

Hypothesizing involves using ideas that one already has, from past experience, to attempt to explain or give a reason for some new event or observation. 'I think the windows are steaming up because it is cold outside', is a hypothesis explaining an observation; 'seeds grow best in the dark' is expressed as a statement, or proposition, but it contains a hypothesis (that darkness helps seeds to grow). A hypothesis can be expressed in a variety of ways; it is not the form but the intention of a statement which indicates whether or not it is a hypothesis. It must attempt to give an explanation. Furthermore, the suggested explanation does not have to be the scientifically accepted one, nor have to be complete as long as it is consistent with the evidence available at the time.

Scientific hypotheses are testable by investigation. To test them the first step is to use them to make a prediction ('if we put these seeds in the dark then they will grow better than seeds in the light'). Sometimes, the prediction is made at the same time and so the hypothesis is expressed as a prediction; indeed, there is a common misunderstanding that hypotheses have to be in an 'if ... then ...' form. Hypothesis and prediction are separate in function though often coincident in use. In the STAR list, prediction is included as part of data interpretation, since predictions can be made on the basis of data as well as following from hypotheses.

Children's ability to suggest hypotheses is rooted in identifying a factor or feature as a possible cause, even if at this early stage the suggestion does not indicate how the factor could operate in a causal way and may, indeed, be an unlikely cause (although seen as relevant to the child). There is this germ of a hypothesis in statements such as 'leaves fall off the trees when the wind blows too strongly for them to hold on'. An advance is to suggest an explanation which is based on a more relevant concept; 'leaves fall off the trees when it gets cold' – even though the mechanism of how the cold affects the trees is not suggested.

Ability to hypothesize at a more advanced level is indicated by an attempt to suggest a mechanism, even though it may not be correct. Here the child is realizing that an explanation in terms of just naming a relevant feature is not enough, the way in which it operates is part of the explanation: 'we found lots of snails at the bottom of the wall because it was damp there and snails need the moisture'.

A further advance in hypothesizing is the recognition that there may be more than one explanation. An example of this is found in the explanations which children gave to the question of why snails were not found in a particular garden (Schilling, 1990); 'There was either something in the garden they didn't like or there wasn't something they did like'. Other answers of the, 'it could have been winter, or the birds might have eaten them' kind, show the same open-mindedness to alternative possibilities.

Bringing these indicators together, signs of a child being able to hypothesize at different levels are:

- mentions one relevant feature (at least) in attempting an explanation;
- gives an explanation in terms of a relevant concept (even if only by naming it);
- gives an explanation in terms of a mechanism involving a concept (correct or incorrect);
- gives an explanation (in terms of a mechanism) which fits evidence and is consistent with science concepts;
- gives, or acknowledges, more than one possible explanation.

Planning

We think of planning as an exercise carried out on paper and preceding the action which is being mapped out. But the ability to do this develops out of a more limited planning, which may not be written down and which may not anticipate more than a few first actions. Young children tend to 'think through action', and only when the result of an action is found do they consider the next step. Gradually, experience enables them to anticipate what will happen at each step, and be able to think further ahead. Thus an early indication of planning is the identification of a starting point which will provide a relevant first step in an investigation.

Planning at a more advanced level demands more steps to be carried out. These will include deciding what is to be investigated (what are we changing or comparing or looking at?); what other things should be kept the same (controlled) so that fair tests or comparisons can be made; what should be measured or compared to find the result; and how can the measurements or observations be made with accuracy.

In the APU surveys of eleven year olds, carried out between 1980 and 1984, it was found that children found certain of these aspects of planning more difficult than others. Deciding what was to be changed (the independent variable), was part of planning which children were more able to do than the identification of what was likely to change and so should be measured or compared (the dependent variable). They were usually able to identify what not to change (the variables to be controlled) if they could say what was to be changed (Harlen, 1986).

All these, then, are features of planning which show some development of this skill. They are summarized in the following indicators:

- identifies a starting point or initial action relevant to the investigation;
- identifies the appropriate variable to change or the things to compare;
- identifies at least one variable which should be kept the same for a fair test;
- identifies all relevant variables to control for a fair test;
- identifies an appropriate variable to measure or compare.

Measuring

Measuring is an important skill which helps to provide the evidence for developing ideas that describe relationships in quantitative terms, rather than just qualitatively. For example, children can conclude from drawing shadows on the ground at different times of the day, without measuring, that shadows of the sun become longer as time goes on after midday (this is a qualitative relationship). But if they measure the shadows they will be able to say how much longer shadows become (a quantitative relationship), and it would be possible to find out if this difference changes from one time of the year to another. Thus ideas can be refined to a greater degree when observations are refined by measurement.

Even when the aim of an investigation is only to find a qualitative relationship (of the 'which ball is the best bouncer' type), making comparisons is aided by measurements – to find how high each ball bounces, for example, so that these heights can be compared. In such cases, the units need not be standard centimetres or metres; they could be the number of bricks from the bottom of a wall or some other arbitrary unit. The important point is that a consistent unit is used throughout.

As mentioned in the last section, deciding what to measure is closely related to planning. A child who has developed skills in using measurement will plan to measure something which is measureable with the equipment and instruments available. For example, it is not feasible to measure a time interval of less than a second with the instruments the children will be able to use, so it would be pointless to plan to measure the time it takes a stone to fall through 10 cm of water. This feature will have to be taken into account in the planning.

Another aspect of measurement skill closely related to planning is deciding the range over which measurements ought to be taken. For example, in investigating the influence of a model boat's sail area on its speed, the question arises as to whether it is enough to compare a large and a small sail area or whether intermediate sizes should also be tested. The aspect of planning here is making enough measurements to be sure whether or not it is the area which is making a difference.

Measurement also involves taking steps to be reasonably sure of each measurement, by checking and repeating it and deciding what to do if it is not the same each time. Primary children do not often do this spontaneously, but it is an important experience basic to understanding that measurements are always uncertain to some degree.

In summary, indicators of a child using these aspects of measurement skill are the following:

- makes comparisons in terms of some quantity which is measured or estimated;
- uses an appropriate unit of measurement, standard or arbitrary;
- chooses the quantity to measure or compare such that reasonable accuracy is possible;
- takes an adequate set of measurements of the relevant variable;
- checks or repeats measurements to improve accuracy.

Interpreting data

Under this broad heading are included finding patterns or associations within data, using these to make predictions and what is commonly called 'drawing conclusions'. All these are included in the term 'interpretation', and all are concerned with relating one piece of data (one piece of information gathered or given), to another, as opposed to leaving them as isolated findings. If children draw up a table of results and leave it at that, or just list their findings, the opportunity to use and develop interpretation skill is missed. If, on the other hand, they notice that one thing changes regularly with another ('the further the lamp is away, the longer the shadow') they are using the skill of interpretation to develop ideas (about how shadows are formed). Thus interpretation has a central role as a process skill which helps concept development.

One of the obstacles to children interpreting data is that they will inevitably have preconceived ideas about the things they are investigating, and there is a tendency to use these ideas rather than the data in drawing conclusions. A key aspect of interpretation is, therefore, the ability (and willingness) to use the data in making an interpretation. Whether or not this has been done may have to be probed by asking children to explain the basis for their prediction or relationship (a guess, or 'I knew it already', or 'because we found . . .').

As this process skill develops, children not only use the data they have in making an interpretation, but realize that while this may fit what they have, it is possible that it may not fit other data, so they test it out. Here is the germ of recognizing all conclusions as tentative, which is important to preserve in scientific activity at all levels.

In summary, the indicators of children using interpretation skill are:

- offers an interpretation related to the data (rather than preconceived ideas) even if the relationship is only loose;
- gives an interpretation based on all available data;
- checks an interpretation against new data;
- bases the interpretation of data on patterns or relationships;
- justifies predictions from data in terms of observed relationships.

Recording and Communicating

Recording and communicating have several crucial roles in science activities, and are regarded here in this light as part of the learning experience and not something added on after the event. During their activities, children become so involved in what they are doing that they often forget to keep notes and records of what is happening and so rely on their memory. Their record is then made at the end of the activity, and has a limited value for the conduct of the activity. Nevertheless, it can serve a useful purpose of communicating to others, if it is to go into a classbook, for example. It then has some value in prompting reflection upon, and ordering of, events in the mind as necessary for writing something down or making a drawing.

As activities become more extended, and particularly when they involve measurements, recording only at the end and relying on memory is not adequate. Then children have to be encouraged to keep records while the work is in progress. Gradually they see the value of this for themselves and will not need to be reminded to do it; they may include the form of record in their planning.

For effective and efficient recording the form of record most useful for the task in hand has to be selected. This, in turn, depends on knowing what forms are available and might be used. Activities which introduce children to the use of tables and to the conventions of representing data on block graphs, charts, flow diagrams, etc., help to develop recording skill. But following directions to use them is not the same as choosing to use them in appropriate circumstances, which is an aspect of this skill to be looked for.

Even though there is particular value in the permanency of a written account of their work, there is always the place for an oral account which can become the basis for a group or whole class discussion. Discussion, as we have said before, is a vital part of the developing of skills and ideas further. For such accounts to serve as useful communication they will recount events in a sequence, give the important, not trivial, details, and take account of what the audience knows about the work. The skill of being able to record and communicate one's work makes it open to the scrutiny of oneself and others, and so is a prerequisite for critical reflection.

These aspects of skill in recording and communicating are brought together in the following list of indicators:

- makes notes or drawings at the end of an investigation;
- makes notes or drawings during an investigation;
- uses tables or other standard framework for recording findings during an investigation;
- provides a reasonably accurate oral account of actions and findings;
- provides a reasonably accurate written account of actions and findings.

Reflecting Critically on Procedures

The process of critical reflection is seen as having a key role in the development of children's thinking. If an investigation stops when the data has been collected and recorded, then a learning opportunity is missed. The chance for children to reflect on what was found is important in terms of the development of their ideas, since it helps them to link up what they have found with other things. Equally as important is to reflect on how the results were found, to consider what else, or what different, might have been done, whether it would have been an improvement (perhaps to try it if circumstances allow) and generally to expand the range of possible approaches available for further work. The deliberate attempts to use each activity as a learning experience in the process of investigation is very helpful to children's scientific development.

Yet reflection is not something which children appear to engage in very readily without encouragement; they need help to develop skills of critical reflection. A discussion of the 'fairness' of their tests often gives opportunity for children to adopt a critical stance in a positive way in relation to details of their work. 'It would have been fairer to have given the same amount of each food,' said Kevin, after trying to tempt mealworms with different foods, which had been offered in vastly varying quantities (including a whole banana!) in an investigation to see which they preferred. 'I think it would have been better if I'd measured more than one stem of cow parsley in each place,' commented a nine year old who had been looking for differences in plant growth on each side of a tall hedge near the school. He added, 'And I could have measured other plants as well.'

The process of reflection begins from some form of communication or recording and thus depends to some extent on these skills. For teachers, however, it is useful to keep the two separately in mind, for critical reflection on a report has to be conducted so that it does not deter children from describing openly and fully what they have done.

These points lead to the following indicators of critical reflections:

- takes part willingly in reviewing what has been done, even if comments are only justifications;
- admits the possibility of alternative approaches or features of the investigation;
- suggests ways of improving details of the investigation;
- considers the pros and cons of alternative approaches or features;
- offers criticism of the approach chosen or may start again with a different approach.

The present chapter has outlined the rationale for the process skills used by the STAR project, and given some indication of the place of process skills in primary science. The place of observation in assessing the use of these skills can be seen clearly from the comparison of STAR skills and National Curriculum Attainment Target 1. How can we determine whether a child can ask questions and suggest ideas of the 'how', 'why' and 'what will happen if' variety unless some form of observation is employed? The following chapter addresses the issue of systematic classroom observation, and discusses several methods of collecting quantitative data.

3

Observing the Classroom Systematically

In Chapter 1 we discussed, in very general terms, the various approaches available to teachers for observing pupil behaviour in the classroom. We saw that these available approaches could be broken down into two major strategies according to whether they emphasized the quantitative or qualitative aspects of the pupils' activities. In this chapter we shall consider, in greater detail, the measures used by systematic observers, that is, those who place the emphasis on the collection of quantitative data. For readers faced with the demands of the National Curriculum, the most effective approach when teaching science in the primary school might be, initially at least, to use the Science Processes Observation Categories (SPOC) developed by the research team. It is hoped, however, that as teachers grow more confident in the use of the methodology, they will begin to experiment either by modifying the SPOC system, or by developing their own observational schedule which they feel will be more appropriate for the needs of their pupils and classroom. Accordingly, the first part of this chapter will provide a review of the main characteristics of the systematic observation approach including the different types of observation systems, methods of coding and analysis. For the interested reader, a more thorough discussion of these issues can be found in Galton (1987b) and Croll (1986). A large number of observation schedules can be found in Simon and Boyer (1970) or Galton (1978). The latter is more suitable for British primary classrooms with their emphasis on informality.

SYSTEMATIC OBSERVATION

In Chapter 1 we defined the main characteristics of a systematic observation schedule to be:

- the capture of a behavioural event by an observer;

- the coding of this event;
- the subsequent analysis of these events in search of patterns.

Rosenshine and Furst (1973) were two of the earliest researchers to sub-divide systematic observation schedules into two types of system. The first type they defined as a category system in which all the exchanges taking place could be coded under one of a number of discrete categories. For example, a simple category system, for observing conversation in the classroom, might consist of five subdivisions:

Teacher talks with pupil(s)
Teacher talks with another adult
Another adult talks with pupil(s)
Pupil(s) talks with other pupil(s)
Silence or non-verbal interaction.

With such a system any behaviour which did not involve either the pupils talking to each other, or to the teacher, or to another adult (such as a parent), would be categorized as silence or non-verbal interaction. The latter category is therefore a very general one which allows all behaviour other than conversation to be recorded. The best-known example of a category system is that of the Flanders Interaction Analysis Categories (FIAC) which consists of ten sub-headings consisting of seven involving teacher talk, two involving pupil talk, and one general category, labelled silence or confusion.

The sub-divisions within a category system of this kind are, however, necessarily broad. Of the five categories listed above, that describing pupils talking with other pupils could include all kinds of conversation. A pupil might be asking a question of the other pupils on his or her table, or telling the others the answer to a mathematical problem on a worksheet, or requesting someone to pass a piece of equipment, for example a stop watch in a scientific experiment. An observer who was interested in these kinds of interactions would find it difficult to devise a category system which included the necessary number of sub-divisions for teacher and adult talk, as well as for conversations between pupils. Either the number of categories would become impossibly large, or the number of decisions which an observer needed to make would increase the likelihood of mistakes in the coding, and so introduce an element of unreliability into the procedure. Observers who wish to work in this way therefore devise a second type of observation schedule – the sign system in which only a selected number of behavioural events are recorded.

Sign systems are more specific and the sub-categories tend to be more complex, so that an observer needs a longer time in which to recognize and code the various behaviours. An example of a sign system is the Science Teaching Observation Schedule (STOS) devised by Eggleston, Galton and Jones (1975). In one part of the schedule, the observer has to decide the nature of the questions asked by the teacher. The questions can be such that they require pupils to recall facts, solve problems (either closed or open ended), design experiments, hypothesize or make inferences on the basis of previous observations. At times, observers find it very difficult to distinguish between a pupil who is making an inference on the basis of available data, and a pupil who engages in speculation which goes beyond the data but which can, nevertheless, be tested by the design of a further experiment. Because such activities were rather rare during science lessons, an extended time unit of three minutes was used in the original STOS version. Observers were only required to record these sub-categories once and only once during any time interval. An observer who, for example, recorded a question which was answered by factual information, could then forget this category for the rest of the three minute time unit and concentrate instead on identifying occurrences of the remaining more complex behaviours. In practice, however, most observation schedules consist of a mixture of category and sign systems so that it is possible, for example, to estimate as a proportion of the total behaviour, the percentage of teacher talk and pupil talk, while at the same time carrying out a more detailed analysis of specific elements occurring during teachers' and pupils' conversations.

Rosenshine and Furst (1973) also make an important distinction between low inference and high inference measures within systematic observation. They include as low inference measurement all categories within an observation system which record specific identifiable behaviours such as, 'pupil sits in his/her place', or 'is mobile', or is 'out of base' (e.g. is at another pupils' table), or is 'engaged elsewhere' in the classroom (as when washing equipment at a sink). High inference behaviours are those where the criteria are less specific and where often a global assessment is made of the pupil's behaviour. The most obvious example of a high inference system is a rating schedule where the observer may be asked to infer certain attributes of a teacher such as warmth and sociability, or of the pupils' interest in learning or their level of co-operation with other pupils. Here the observer is required to watch the teacher or the pupil over a period of time, and then to integrate these impressions into a global assessment of the behaviour of the person under observation. In some systems such as the one used by Powell (1985), to describe 'the teachers' craft', observations of specific categories were made, and these were then combined into an overall rating of the kind described above.

In practice, most observation systems will contain some sub-categories which are clearly more inferential than others, in that they are more ambiguous and require an observer to combine a number of impressions in recording a single judgement. Thus, for example, in the ORACLE study of pupil behaviour (Galton *et al.*, 1980) observers had to record whether, when a pupil was interacting with another pupil or group of pupils, the group consisted of entirely one sex or was mixed. Observers found it a relatively straightforward task to decide whether the pupils involved were either all boys or all girls, and to categorize the interaction as between single or mixed sex according to the gender of the pupil under observation. However, other categories such as 'responding to internal stimuli' (RIS) were clearly more inferential. A pupil, although gazing out of a window, could be thinking about the problem on which he or she was engaged. An observer would be likely to code such an event according to what had taken place either directly before or after this behaviour. If, for example, immediately after a period of staring out of the window, the pupil began to write furiously the observer would be unlikely to regard staring out of the window, in this particular case, as distraction. On the other hand, if the pupil broke off from looking out of the window to engage in social chat and laughter with a neighbour, then the observer would be more likely to use the (RIS) category.

METHODS OF OBSERVATION

It is not always necessary for the observer to record events 'live' in the classroom. Galton (1987b) lists a number of ways in which a permanent record of classroom events can be obtained, allowing an observer to conduct a subsequent analysis under less pressurized circumstances. The two most frequently used approaches are the use of tape and video recorders. There are advantages and disadvantages to such methods. With the availability of moderately cheap, hand-held video cameras, the collection of video records has become increasingly popular as a way of observing classroom events. The main advantage is that they supply a permanent visual and sound record which can be played and replayed and from which critical sections can be edited. This increases the likelihood of agreement between different observers in the subsequent analysis of these critical episodes. Against the advantage of a permanent record, however, must be set the highly selective representation by the camera. A category such as 'target pupil is interested in another pupil's work' could be difficult to code if the camera was focusing directly on the pupil, since the viewer would be uncertain whether the target pupil was looking elsewhere in the classroom, at what was happening between the teacher and another pupil, or was simply staring vacantly into space. In an attempt to overcome such difficulties, two cameras are sometimes used, one focused on the teacher or pupil, and the other providing a general view of the classroom so that individual interactions are placed in a wider context. Such complex arrangements, however, create potential sources of distraction for both pupils and the teacher, so that what may be gained in reliability may be lost in validity in that the behaviour of the pupils and the teacher is no longer typical.

Tape recording, by itself, does not offer the same advantages as video tape, although a modification used by Adelman and Walker (1975) introduced visual cues in the form of stop frame photography with the camera synchronized to the sound. Both tape and video recording do require considerable back-up resources. It is estimated that an hour's tape recording takes up to fifteen hours of a typist's time, particularly if the typist is not using a tape recorder with a slowed-down speech facility. When the transcription is finally produced, it is usually found that much of the material is irrelevant to the analysis being undertaken. There are also difficulties in recording and a tendency for pupils, particularly when engaged in small group work, to react untypically in the presence of the microphone.

More importantly, when an observer records events 'as they happen', the presence of the observer in the classroom, particularly over a period of time, has the advantage that it enables him or her to appreciate the shared understandings which exist between the pupils and the teacher, so that certain behaviours can more easily be interpreted in the light of this experience. This is particularly true when the investigation concerns aspects of the classroom climate where private jokes – such as the strawberries incident recorded by Adelman and Walker (1975) – are a common feature. For these reasons, it is generally better, at least in the initial stages of an investigation, to make use of permanent records only when the focus of interest is the children's language involving, for example, the logical processes of discourse. Readers who are interested in this aspect of conversation should find Edwards and Westgate (1987) particularly helpful.

CODING AND ANALYSIS

Various methods exist for recording behaviours and these are discussed in some detail by Croll (1986). The most usual approach involves the use of time sampling methods as in the ORACLE study. There observers recorded pupil and teacher behaviours, as they happened, at twenty-five second intervals. Other schedules have used shorter periods as, for example, in the PRISMS project (Galton and Patrick, 1990) where the time interval was reduced, for some categories, to five seconds.

The length of time interval depends on a number of factors, chiefly the complexity of the system and the requirement that the observer is able to record smoothly without stress. Above all, the resulting analysis should give a picture of the classroom which, in the observer's view, has face validity, that is, it matches the overall impression of the observer as to the sequence of events in a particular classroom relative to others in the study. For example, an observer might be looking at the extent to which children are required to answer questions from the teacher that require a hypothesis on their part. During trials of the system, the observer might select several classes where, on impression alone, it seemed that levels of hypothesizing varied. During the initial use of the observation schedule, the observer would try various time intervals and seek a compromise between reducing stress yet recording sufficient occasions that the rank order of frequency of hypothesizing between different teachers was in accord with the initial impression as to the extent of enquiry in each of the classrooms.

In some cases, the observer may attempt a continuous record over a short period. An observer, for example, may be interested in the ratio of teacher initiated talk (Category A) to pupil initiated talk (Category B). The schedule would, therefore, consist of one minute rows divided into sixty sub-sections, each representing a second. The observer would code 'A' at the start of a teacher utterance, and then code 'B' at the point when the teacher stopped talking and the pupil began either to respond or to initiate further discussion. If these categories had been used in a time-sampling system, they would have been given an 'estimated' ratio of teacher–pupil talk, where accuracy depended on the extent to which the time interval provided a representative sample of the total behaviours. In a continuous record, the ratio, apart from observer error, provides an accurate representation. An example of this method, which obviously demands considerable effort on the part of the observer, can be found in the account of The Teacher's Day (Hillsum and Caine, 1971). With this type of recording it is obviously necessary that events do not change very rapidly. In the study of The Teacher's Day, for example, very broad categories were used such as playtime, marking and assembly (see Croll (1986) for an extended discussion). A modification of this procedure is to use larger elements of time, say one minute intervals, and simply record with a tick whenever a particular event of interest takes place. This technique, event recording, has often been used to distinguish between higher order and lower order levels of questioning, for example.

Finally, it is very important to check that a sample of behaviour is representative of both the curriculum activity and of the composition of the class. For example, given that there are differences between boys and girls in their attitudes to science, it would be important to make certain that boys and girls were represented in the same proportion as the total numbers in the classroom. The actual choice of a particular boy or girl should be random, and can easily be done by drawing names from a hat. At other times, it may be necessary to have a more complicated sampling frame. We may, for example, not only require a balance between boys and girls, but also between pupils in the top, middle and bottom range of ability. This was certainly necessary in the ORACLE study, because critics of primary practice had alleged that 'bright pupils received less attention from the teacher than those of limited ability'.

However, those who carry out observational studies often pay less attention to balancing different curriculum activities. In the primary classroom, for example, some activities require pupils to be more mobile than others. In science, it would be unfair to compare the performance of one pupil while he or she was conducting an experiment with another who was seen while he or she was writing up the results. If such differences are important, then an observer should record the nature of the activity taking place at the time when the observation was taking place. At the end of the observation, it is then possible to make certain that all pupils have been seen for approximately the same period of time while performing similar activities. The easiest way to achieve this is to put the pupils to be observed (the targets) in a random order, and do a small number of observations on each target rather than concentrating on one pupil for a particular length of time before moving on to the next.

In summary, therefore, observation systems will usually consist of a range of high inference and low inference categories. For complex activities, of the kind generally associated with science teaching, a sign system will mostly be used, during which the observer concentrates on a limited number of behaviours and ignores others that are not thought relevant to the investigation. The usual method of recording these observations will be through a time-sampling procedure in which the observer samples behaviours at discrete intervals of time. The length of these time intervals will be decided on a 'trial and error' basis in order to achieve a compromise between an accurate representation of the totality of events under investigation and a manageable situation for the observer. Care must also be taken to ensure that the sample of pupils observed is representative of the class, and also that each pupil is observed across approximately the same range of curriculum activities. This is usually accomplished by drawing up a prearranged order, whereby each pupil is observed in rotation for a short period rather than observing an individual for an extended period. In the ORACLE study, for example, there were eight target pupils in each class, and each target was observed over five, twenty-five second intervals (approximately two and a half minutes) in rotation. When using the pupil observation schedule, each individual could, therefore, receive around fifteen minutes' observation during the course of a day.

ASSESSING THE EFFECTIVENESS OF PUPIL PERFORMANCE

In Chapter 1, a view of learning was put forward whereby, through the use of what were identified in Chapter 2 as the science process skills, children are able to reconstruct existing ideas in order to make better sense of the world around them. While it was accepted that the extent to which these process skills can be used to bring about greater understanding will be restricted by the child's existing knowledge, it was argued that it was important that the children themselves should see the need to adopt new ideas rather than simply being told to do so by the teacher. The development of concepts and the development of process skills are therefore closely linked and highly interdependent. To engage fruitfully in this scientific activity whereby ideas about the world can be changed, children also need to develop certain attitudes such as curiosity, flexibility and open-mindedness. In order to provide suitable learning experiences so that children can progress in this way, a teacher will need to make certain judgements based upon the pupil's performance. We shall term such judgements 'assessment'.

There are a number of important issues involved when deciding on the form of assessment to be used. In particular, we need to take account of the validity and reliability of the methods, particularly if they are to be used either for selection or to report publicly on the child's progress or the schools' performance. In its simplest terms, validity means that our assessment of the task that the child performs is a true measure of the knowledge, skill or attitude which we are claiming to assess. Reliability, on the other hand, is a measure of consistency and estimates the extent to which any single assessment is an accurate measure of the child's capability. Different methods of assessment tend either to achieve improved reliability at the expense of validity, or to be more valid measures while appearing to give less consistent results. For example, written tests can be made highly reliable so that a child's performance on one occasion is very similar to that on the next. Their validity is, however, often strongly criticised, because in answering such questions, the pupil relies heavily on what are termed 'general study skills' of comprehension and organizing information, rather than the particular skill or concept that the question was designed to assess. Some critics such as Holt (1964) argue, for example, that testing is not 'necessary' or useful or even 'excusable', and that 'at best it does more harm than good' since 'it hinders, distorts and corrupts the learning process' (Holt, 1964, p. 51). Others, however, would argue equally strongly that ways can be found to improve the validity of written tests, as in the development of project related assessments, such as The Walled Garden, described in an earlier volume in this series (Schilling *et al.*, 1990). Here, the assessments are built into the general work activity within the classroom, so that to the pupil they seem part of normal learning rather than a special, untypical activity. Such procedures, however, pose problems, since by constructing the assessment within a normal planned sequence of classroom tests, an added premium is placed upon the child's comprehension skills and powers of concentration. This factor influenced the recommendation of the Task Group on Assessment and Testing (TGAT) that the assessment of a child's capabilities should be based not upon one single application of a particular method, but on the aggregate of the results from a number of different approaches (TGAT, 1987, para. 88–90).

It is for this reason that the use of observation as a means of assessing a pupil's performance is so important and, therefore, such a valuable technique. Such use assumes that the various categories of behaviour can be defined in a relatively unambiguous way, so that they are low inference measures. The categories are then more likely to have a high degree of face validity, i.e. different teachers will agree that the behaviours observed and coded within a category are good indicators of the child's performance in respect of a particular process skill. While the reliability of such observations may not be so high as that of a written test, improvement can be effected by teachers coming together to observe and code the same event. They then discuss any differences in coding until the ambiguities in the interpretation of the various categories have been either resolved or reduced. Unlike a test, which is a single measure of the pupil's performance, an observation session can provide a series of 'repeated measures' of a pupil's competence. These observations can then either be aggregated to provide an 'average score', or the most favourable value in a set of observations can be recorded, on the grounds that it represents the maximum capability of a pupil in a given circumstance.

In a class of thirty children, however, there are clear, practical advantages in using a written assessment rather than an observation schedule. In an earlier discussion, it was pointed out that in the ORACLE project it was only possible, in a sample of eight pupils, to record between twelve and fifteen minutes' observation over the course of a day. Naturally, these observations were carried out across the whole curriculum and not just during science activities. In observing science process skills, the total time available would be only a fraction of the whole day. If a teacher was to engage in detailed systematic observation of the whole class during these science sessions, there would be little time for anything else. The TGAT report recognizes this problem and suggests a moderation strategy (TGAT, 1987, para. 78–80) that could be adapted for individual classes. Teachers could design tasks, which required pupils to exercise not more than two specific process skills. On the basis of general unstructured observation, they could carry out high inference ratings on all the pupils using scales of the type developed by Harlen *et al.* during the Progress in Learning Science project (Schools Council, 1977). These high inference assessments could then be compared with the results of standard assessment tasks. Only in cases where there was a serious mismatch between the assessments on a pupil would further detailed observation be carried out.

This procedure could be carried out as follows. Let us suppose that the teacher rated the children's observed performance using a five-point scale of the kind developed by Harlen *et al.* in the Progress in Learning Science project (Schools

Council, 1977), and that the pupil also had an aggregated score based on various kinds of written Standard Assessment Tasks (SAT) such that a maximum value of twenty was possible. Assuming that these latter SAT scores were reasonably distributed, a teacher might divide them into five categories, each consisting of five mark intervals. Those pupils whose teacher rating differed from that of the SAT rating by more than one category (for example, a pupil might be rated '3' by the teacher but have an aggregate score of five marks on the SAT, equivalent to category '1'), would then be selected for further observation.

There is another way in which observation can be used to improve the quality of teachers' assessments. Under normal classroom conditions, a teacher's aim will be to set tasks such that the majority of pupils will eventually succeed in completing them satisfactorily. To achieve this aim, the teacher will come to the aid of a pupil whenever he or she appears to be having difficulties. The kind of help necessary is therefore not only an indication of the success of the 'match' between the cognitive demand of the task and the child's ability, but can also be an indicator of the pupil's progress if the pattern of help can be identified.

In science, for example, when pupils are working on practical problems involving designing experiments, a teacher might have to help pupils (a) to identify correctly what features need to vary (the independent variables), (b) which variables need to be held constant if they are not to affect the investigation, (c) what measure should be investigated (the dependent variable), (d) how such measurements should be collected, and (e), analysed. A pupil who could complete all these steps successfully unaided would have grasped the idea of 'fair' testing. By recording the letter (a) to (e) according to the kind of help and support required, a teacher could build up a picture, over time, of the way in which the pupil's thinking was developing.

Systematic observation is also seen as an essential component of the appraisal process. In a recent report on the evaluation of the School Teacher Appraisal Pilot Study, the evaluators concluded that 'at times classroom observation has been seen by some teachers as being the whole of the appraisal' (Bradley, 1989, p. 19). There was a view among some teachers who took part in the evaluation pilot study, that systematic observation is best used as part of a developmental programme under the control of the teacher concerned, rather than as part of the more formal appraisal procedure. Teachers generally found it preferable to note the atmosphere and 'get a general view of what was happening' (Bradley, 1989, p. 21).

Part of this evident reluctance of teachers to use systematic observation probably stems from its association with past studies of teacher effectiveness in which the sole outcome measure consisted of the pupils' scores on standardized tests. Such 'process–product' studies have been used extensively in the United States to develop 'direct instruction' teaching prescriptions (Rosenshine, 1987), which have been used increasingly by many local school boards for accountability purposes. The 'process–product' model was advocated as long ago as 1936 by Barr, who argued that one way of improving the quality of teaching was to distinguish between effective and ineffective teachers on the basis of certain outcomes; to observe classes where these outcomes were achieved; and compare the behaviour of their teachers with others from classes where the outcomes were not achieved. Process–product studies do not, therefore, have to be restricted by defining effectiveness solely in terms of standardized tests. An appraisal might, for example, be interested in looking at the behaviour of different teachers in science classes where pupils raised questions continually about the results of their experiments, as against classes where children did not. In Chapter 1, for example, we described a teacher who had concluded, on the basis of her observations during the STAR project, that the children could not engage in challenging activities without her presence. She, therefore, reorganized her lessons so that science was done not as a whole class, but by groups in rotation. She then spent considerable amounts of time with the group who were doing science, directing and helping them with their experiments. In the STAR project, however, the research team came across many examples of teachers who were able to find ways of encouraging pupils to work on similar experiments without such guidance. In this particular case, a process–product study would have been useful in helping to generate possible reasons why the first teacher was unsuccessful in using a less directed approach. It might be, for example, that the pupil's previous experiences had been limited, or the classroom climate developed by the teacher was not supportive of this independent style of learning.

Using a process–product approach in this way argues for an appraisal programme based upon a developmental approach. By this we mean that as a result of an appraisal interview, based upon unstructured observation, a teacher might identify areas of concern within his or her practice, and set out a list of priorities for future development. As part of this programme of development, a teacher would agree to engage in investigation of his or her present practice. Part of this programme could involve the collection of observation data about specific aspects of the teacher's classroom behaviour.

Within one school, for example, a headteacher in an appraisal interview with several staff identified as a common problem the lack of time available for helping children. It was agreed with the teachers concerned – one with a class of nine year olds and one with a class of six year olds – that they would carry out an investigation in their own classrooms on the way that time was used. The junior teacher decided on an informal means of observation and recorded at the end of day, in a diary, the times when she remembered wanting more time with a child, and what had prevented her from giving that particular pupil more attention. Most of the cases noted involved outside interventions over which she had no control. For example, the school had an 'open door' policy of inviting parents into the classroom, and on numerous occasions parents arrived and interrupted a lesson in order to provide information about their child, such as a visit to the dentist the next day. Other interruptions occurred when pupils from other classes came into the classroom bringing messages from the headteacher or from other colleagues. At the suggestion of the headteacher, she also collected information from the pupils by asking them to complete a card at the end of each day which listed three occasions when they had wanted her attention and described what the teacher was doing so that she was prevented from joining them.

The infant teacher, however, realized that it would not be possible to use this method with the younger children. She therefore decided on a programme of direct observation. Sitting down with the class, she identified all the things for which they needed the teacher. She then constructed an observation schedule in the form of pictures showing the teacher hearing a child read, helping with sums, talking to the class, and even telling a pupil off! During one week, whenever one of the pupils wanted the teacher, they ticked the column with the appropriate picture at the top which indicated why the teacher was unavailable. Without knowing it, therefore, the teacher had devised a simple sign system using an event sampling strategy. Combining the data, as a class exercise on the computer, the children drew bar charts showing the frequency of each event. It was fairly easy to demonstrate that for the teacher to satisfy every pupil's request for help would only leave around one second of time available for each pupil during a lesson. It was also clear that the teacher would need to reduce the time given over to hearing children read, and also to marking children's arithmetic computations. Accordingly, together with the class the teacher drew up a series of rules which enabled pupils to book an extended period of five minutes with the teacher. The rules indicated what the other pupils should do so that a child's five minutes of the teacher's time was not interrupted. These rules included checking one's answers with a neighbour (a long discussion here on the difference between copying and learning things from each other) and, in the last resort, getting on with some alternative activity, until the teacher was free, when help could not be found elsewhere. A consultant was employed to observe the levels of engagements on children while the teacher was having these longer conversations with particular pupils. It was found, once the rules had been mastered, that the levels of engagement among pupils were uniformally high – higher than found in a typical class during the ORACLE study, for example. The success of these observations with the younger children led the teacher with the class of nine year olds to involve her pupils in a similar observation study to clarify the differences between her perceptions of what has recently been referred to as 'evaporated time', and those of her pupils.

CLASSROOM OBSERVATION AND TEACHER FEEDBACK

The use of observation as part of either formal appraisal of a programme of self-development, as in the above example, will depend for its effectiveness on the kinds of feedback provided. The evaluators of the School Teacher Appraisal Pilot Study (Bradley, 1989, p. 20) found that, where observation was included as part of a formal appraisal process, all the local authorities concerned advocated a 'clinical supervision' model consisting of preparation, then observation and finally feedback. It was considered essential that feedback should be given within forty-eight hours of observation taking place. In most cases, preliminary discussion occurred immediately after the end of observation, and this was followed by a more detailed discussion the next day.

Among the weaknesses in the feedback process were criticisms that those carrying out the appraisal sometimes tended to be 'too soft'. This is perhaps a surprising finding, but is reinforced in the evaluation report by the comment that 'appraisees have very high expectations of them', i.e. the appraisers. Those carrying out the appraisal must, therefore, demonstrate a satisfactory level of skill in observation in order to command the respect of those who are submitting themselves to the experience. It is helpful when reporting back observations to teachers, to display this data in the form of bar charts or pie charts, rather than simply recorded percentages. When presenting this data, it is important to try to do so in terms which are not overtly 'value laden'.

Having presented the data as objectively as possible, it is then important to listen to the teachers' explanations and to include evidence of 'active listening' by providing short, friendly comments such as, 'that's interesting', or 'do go on'. The person giving the feedback tries to avoid questioning the teacher's response, as if in a cross examination, by attempting to interpret or to analyse the teacher's reflection on their observed practice. Such comments can imply the appraiser feels that he or she is wiser and, from this position of superiority, can see other reasons for the teacher's response. Offering solutions or advice, on the other hand, also defeats the whole purpose of the appraisal exercise since the teacher, by accepting such advice, is then freed from any responsibility for future actions. 'After all', he or she can then say, 'I only did what was suggested'. Finally, it is important to get an agreed, preferably written, statement, of the conclusions, if any, which result from the discussion and the positive steps which it is agreed should be taken in future. The latter, if at all possible, should include further observation.

In situations where a programme of self-development is undertaken and one teacher is acting as a consultant to another, there is less restriction on the consultant introducing suggestions into the discussion since the relationship is more in the nature of a partnership. Listening skills are still important, and where the teacher consultant does make suggestions it is useful to try to make them as a comment on one's own personal experience. Suppose, for example, the teacher and the consultant were discussing an incident where children, when left to their own devices, fooled around and did not work at the task which was to plan a fair experiment. The consultant teacher might say:

> . . . Yes. When children in my class appear reluctant to cooperate on a task like this, I find myself concentrating on this group at the expense of others and this makes me feel frustrated because I am sure that all the other children need equal amounts of attention.

Here the consultant raises the problem of distribution of attention, and attempts to reassure the teacher by indicating that this is a common problem by first describing similar behaviour, by second recounting the concrete effect of that behaviour, and third by then relaying to the other teacher the feelings which these events elicited. Having identified a common problem, the consultant then needs to make sure that the teacher really wants his or her help. The consultant might therefore continue,

> I have been doing some reading and thinking about all of this, and I'd like to share my ideas with you and get your response.

Having put these ideas forward, in this case a need to break down the dependency of the children and to create a classroom climate where risk of failure is acceptable, the consultant teacher should be prepared for his colleague, initially, to resist this view and to express reservations. In response, statements such as:

'I see. It doesn't fit your experience.' or
'Ah! It doesn't make sense to you.'

send a message to the teacher that you are interested in a partnership of ideas and are not simply trying to force your opinion upon him or her. The aim of such discussion should be, as far as possible, to come up with a second cycle of observation that attempts to test out different possible explanations of the pupils' behaviour. As cooperation develops, it should be possible to agree some basic ground rules for decision making as a result of these observations. Whenever possible, two kinds of explanation should be put forward – one on the basis of the teacher's experience of the particular pupils and the other from the pupils' perspective – by interpreting the observations in terms of one's own experience as an adult learner in similar situations. In the example previously discussed, it would be valuable for the teacher and the consultant to think about in-service activities which they had attended where they had been put into groups to solve a challenging problem and their personal reactions to this challenge.

When using observations to assess pupil learning there are many similarities between the role of the consultant with a colleague and a teacher with a pupil. There is evidence to suggest that in the primary school, children's self-esteem tends to be bound up with pleasing their teachers by providing them with the answers they require (Galton, 1989). Pupils of low ability in particular will, when faced with challenging tasks or where there may be more than one correct answer or procedure, tend to adopt a state of what has been termed 'learnt helplessness', rather than risk a hypothesis which might be rejected by their peers or the teacher. In such circumstances, it is no answer for the teacher to tell children 'that they will learn by their mistakes'. Pollard (1985) describes very clearly how children adopt 'avoidance strategies' to reduce the possibility of getting things wrong in such situations. In these circumstances, teachers need to be extremely careful that they are not trapped into offering suggestions too early. Body language has been found to be particularly important in such situations. One teacher, for example, tended to sit partially facing the table whenever she joined a group and often covered her mouth with her hand while her elbow rested on the edge of the table. The general impression conveyed by this posture was, 'I'm here to listen and not to tell', but the teacher concerned was unaware of doing this until she observed herself on video tape.

The actual approach used when providing feedback will depend on the purposes of the assessment. If the assessment is formative, then the main purpose of the feedback is to convey to pupils 'what has been and what remains to be achieved' (TGAT, 1987, para. 37). In this respect, during the post-task interview, the teacher's main aim will be to clarify uncertainties in the observation in order to be certain what the pupil knows and understands. For example, a pupil might have been observed in the process of hypothesizing without having stated the criteria on which the hypothesis was based. Subsequent conversation with the pupil would remove such uncertainties, and enable the teacher to make a more accurate assessment of the child's progress.

However, more recently (Fairbairn, 1988), teachers have begun to place greater emphasis on negotiated assessments where observation is used,

(1) as a means of regular dialogue between teachers and pupils to identify achievement, motivate and to stimulate curriculum review;
(2) to provide a record of achievement which involves the pupil and should be carried out regularly and systematically.

In their evidence to the Task Group on Assessment and Testing, the National Steering Committee for Records of Achievement emphasized the importance of the 'involvement of pupils in their own assessment by means of dialogue between pupils and teachers because the emphasis on such records is primarily diagnostic rather than, in the case of the proposed national assessment scheme, formative'. In this context, therefore, the profile of observed skills is used as a starting point for a dialogue between the pupil and the teacher, with the aim of arriving at a final assessment which stresses the positive achievements of the pupils rather than recording those things which the pupil either was unable to do, or did not attempt. Although, therefore, this kind of record does not fit in with the methods of reporting recommended by TGAT and adopted by SEAC, and this difference of emphasis has led the Secretary of State to cease funding the Records of Achievement programme, the use of negotiated assessment still has an important part to play in the development of pupils' confidence to tackle difficult tasks where there is a high risk of failure. Rowlands (1988), for example, has argued that for children to feel in control of their learning, the teacher needs to adopt the role of critic rather than of evaluator in respect to pupils' achievement. In Rowlands' view, once an activity is underway:

> The teacher's role is then to act as a reflective agent, aiming to help the child identify concerns and needs and also to provide positive yet critical feedback to the student. The child, in turn, critically responds to the teacher's contributions. Neither is 'right' or 'wrong' . . . such invention, even when not successful, is a powerful means for increasing awareness of what skills and knowledge are needed.

> (Rowlands, 1988, p. 131)

In his approach to teaching and learning, Rowlands is echoing Pollard's (1987) view in the same book that 'the thrust of social constructionist arguments seem to suggest that children learn best when they feel in control of their own learning and interpretive sociologists would reinforce this from the motivational point of view'.

To conclude, systematic observation can supply additional evidence about particular pupils' achievement. When used in combination with teacher ratings and more formal written assessments, it adds validity to the profiles of pupils' attainments. The SPOC instrument can be used in this way to validate attainment targets based upon the science process skills. Based on these measures, the importance of formative assessments in demonstrating the current levels of achievement of pupils, should not rule out the use of such profiles for diagnostic puposes. This process can be helped by extending the experience gained at secondary level, in the development of the Records of Achievement approach into the primary school. Based upon a negotiated assessment model, the aims of the Records of Achievement Pilot Study, leading in turn to negotiation in both teaching and learning, not only fit well with the philosophy of primary education but also are consistent with the most recent theories of how children learn (Woods, 1989). The findings from the evaluation projects associated with Records of Achievement Study show that, where this model of teaching and learning has been applied successfully, it has great impact on pupils' motivation and self-esteem. In particular, it appears to have a positive effect on the pupils who experience learning difficulties and who through 'fear of failure' may be reluctant to engage in the exercise of science process skills when these are incorporated into problem-solving practical tasks, where there are no obvious right or wrong answers.

4

The Science Process Observation Categories

In Chapter 3, several methods of observation were described and the merits of each discussed. Here, our concern is the method of recording of observations and the chapter is devoted mainly to a description of the method chosen for the STAR project. The main aim of the observation instrument was to obtain information relating to discussion about the eight process skills which have been identified earlier by Wynne Harlen – observing, interpreting, hypothesizing, planning, measuring, recording, raising questions and critically reflecting. The instrument developed was called the Science Process Observation Categories, subsequently known as SPOC.

The most accurate method of recording observations is to use a continuous recording schedule. A typical schedule might consist, for example, of a number of one minute units, each minute subdivided into six, ten-second intervals. Each category of behaviour is numbered. The observer enters the category number on the schedule at the appropriate second in which the behaviour begins, and draws a vertical line followed by the number of the new category at the appropriate point on the schedule where the behaviour ends. Such a procedure provides a true estimate of both the frequency of an activity and its duration. However, it is clearly limited to observation systems where there are relatively few categories. For more complex systems, time-sampling is used whereby the event is recorded once only during the specific time interval. One-zero time sampling, however, cannot provide evidence of frequency or sequence of behaviour, but merely categorizes the minimum occurrence. It is particularly useful where the categories of behaviour studied occur fairly infrequently. When this situation occurs, the observer is able to code the more usual behaviours at an early point during the time interval, leaving him or her free to concentrate on the more difficult areas of behaviour to be coded. In the Science Teaching Observation Categories system, for example, observers found distinctions between pupils engaging in hypothesizing and interpreting difficult to make, and one-zero time sampling was therefore used. Given the fact that many of the STAR categories involve similar kinds of decisions about behaviour during the science lessons, one-zero time sampling was again preferred in the STAR project.

Initially, two instruments were designed for the observation – one for observation of the teacher and one for observation of the pupils – with the intention of using both instruments in the same lesson. However, the main categories for observation were common to both instruments and therefore it seemed prudent to combine the two together. The teacher observation instrument would have provided a useful picture of the teacher's activity throughout the lesson but, as the ORACLE observation study reported (Galton *et al.*, 1980), the teacher spends very little time with an individual pupil, having thirty or so pupils with whom to interact. Thus the effect of the teacher on an individual pupil was felt to be better assessed by observing teacher-target interaction during the time intervals when the target was the focus of attention.

The SPOC observation instrument was trialled in several schools in order that any problems encountered by the observers in relation to interpretation of categories or procedure of use of the observation schedule could be noted and discussed by the project team. Minor adjustments to category labels and definitions were made until a workable instrument, complete with tight definitions for each category, was derived. The use of several different time intervals were also trialled. A comparison between one-minute continuous observation and two-minute continuous observation intervals suggested that overall results would be similar whichever time was chosen. However, two-minute intervals resulted not only in less work for the observer, but also in less data to be analysed. Use of a time interval longer than two minutes resulted in too many categories being ticked to serve any discriminatory purpose. Taking all these factors into account, the STAR project coded the observations throughout a continuous two-minute interval immediately followed by another two-minute interval.

When using SPOC, one pupil at a time is the focus of the observation and the term 'target pupil' is used to distinguish him or her from other pupils in the class. Details of teacher talk and activity as appropriate to the target on focus are also noted and recorded. It was essential to obtain a fair sample of pupil behaviour within each classroom, controlling for achievement level and pupil gender. The research design, therefore, involved observation, in a random order, of a total of six target pupils from each classroom – one high achiever boy and girl, one middle achiever boy and girl, and one low achiever boy and girl. The STAR project began before the idea of a National Curriculum was first made public, and the range of practice of science teaching in primary schools was known to be wide with some schools engaging in little or no teaching of science, with others having specialists who taught a great deal of science. For this reason, it was decided that pupil achievement levels should be based on teacher assessments of general achievement rather than of science achievement.

When an observer changes focus from one target pupil to another, there is some time spent on locating the new pupil to observe, and to move to a position where the pupil can be seen and heard. To minimize the changeover time, each pupil was observed for two consecutive two-minute intervals and then returned to later in the lesson for a further two two-minute intervals. With this pattern of timing, observation of six pupils for two two-minute intervals would take twenty-four minutes and with a repeat during the same lesson would total forty-eight minutes. With an average lesson time of sixty minutes, there remained twelve minutes for the changeover of observation from one target to another – a rather tight schedule, but one which was considered manageable. The main categories of the observation schedule are:

Seating of target
Number of children
Audience/interaction
Teacher
Curriculum focus of the teacher
Curriculum area of the pupil
Non-talk pupil activity
Dialogue involving the pupil
Other pupil talk
Teacher talk
Non-talk teacher activity

These categories are described in more detail in the following section.

GENERAL ORGANIZATION FEATURES

For each two-minute interval, information relating to the target's seating base (who they were sitting with, the gender mix, and whether paired, grouped or alone), and the audience for the interaction (who the target was talking or listening to), was recorded as a tick in the appropriate box. A majority rule existed. For example, if the target's seating group during the two-minute interval was 'same sex group' for most of the time, then category 2.4 was ticked and the other categories under section 2 left blank. Similarly, for the target's audience (category 4), the audience category which related to the majority of the two minutes was coded as a tick in one of those boxes 4.1 to 4.6. Category 3 recorded the actual number of children in the classroom and the number of children engaged in a science activity during the observation interval. This provided some information about the way the teacher had organized the activities. Consider the example provided in Figure 4.1. The coding shows that the target pupil was sitting in a group of same-sex pupils and talking or listening to the teacher; there were 28 pupils in the classroom of whom only 13 were engaged in science activities. The information indicates that the teacher was not employing a whole class teaching method but, perhaps, some form of group work teaching.

The majority rule also applied to category 5, the teacher's involvement (whether the teacher was listening and watching the target, or actively involved with the target or somewhere else in the classroom engaged with other pupils or busy with

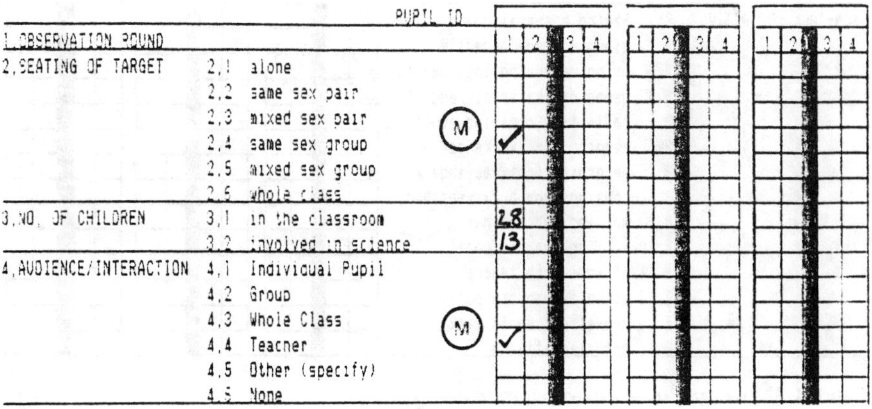

Figure 4.1 *Coding in SPOC categories 2, 3 and 4*

housekeeping activities); also to category 6, the teacher's curriculum focus (may or may not be science if several group activities are going on at the same time); and also to category 7, the curriculum area of the pupil (who might be distracted by other pupils engaged on non-science activities). These categories were designed particularly to obtain information about classes which engage in group work where each group works on a different curriculum area. If the target began to talk to another pupil about a non-science task, then recording of task related categories (categories 8 to 12) ceased until science became the focus once more. Figure 4.2 shows an example of coding where the teacher was engaged with pupils other than the target pupil or his or her group members, but was involved with science, and not a different curriculum area as might have been the case. The target pupil was engaged on a science activity for the majority of the two-minute interval.

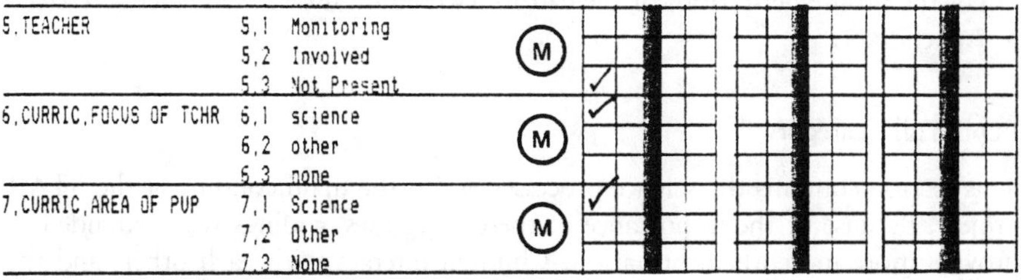

Figure 4.2 *Coding in SPOC categories 5, 6 and 7*

SPOC-CATEGORIES: TASK-RELATED

Non-Talk Pupil Activity (category 8)

The target's activity during the science lesson was coded as a tick in each relevant box. Once a category had been observed during the two-minute interval, it would

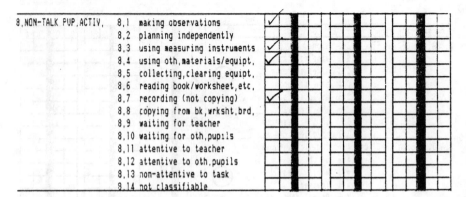

Figure 4.3   *Coding in SPOC category 8*

not be ticked again during the same interval. Several ticks would be likely to appear across categories 8.1 to 8.14. The instrument is, therefore, obtaining minimum occurrence and not a frequency of occurrence of each category. A picture of the regularity of occurrence can be obtained by comparing a set of four two-minute intervals. If a category is ticked in all four intervals, then the activity could be said to have occurred regularly throughout the lesson, and not limited to the beginning or end of the lesson. Conversely, an activity occurring only in the first interval suggests an activity or talk category which might be devoted to the first part of the lesson only. The coding might be made clearer by use of an example. If within a two-minute interval the target pupil was observing the level of floating of three different blocks of wood and making a note of the measured depth of wood left above the water, the codings would be: making observations (8.1), using measuring instruments (8.3), using other materials and equipment (8.4) and recording (8.7). The coding for this example is shown in Figure 4.3.

For the precise definitions of the categories used in SPOC the reader is referred to Appendix 1.

Pupil Talk (category 9)

This section contains the science processes and is the main concern of the STAR project. Because of the importance of these categories, codings were extended to provide more in-depth information. Children interact with each other, and the things a pupil says or does may depend on the web of interchanges which take place between the several members of a group. The codings for this section were, therefore, extended to include descriptions about whether the target pupil was actively engaged in the discussion (coded as 1), or was part of the audience to the discussion (coded as 2), and also to include whether the teacher was involved or not in the interaction (coded T as well as 1 or 2). A priority rule was used here for the observation interval, i.e. if the teacher was involved at any time throughout the two-minutes, then T was coded in the relevant category. If the target pupil was actively engaged in a certain category as well as audience to the same category

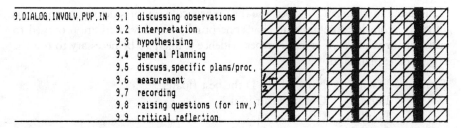

9,DIALOG,INVOLV,PUP,IN	9,1	discussing observations									
	9,2	interpretation									
	9,3	hypothesising									
	9,4	general Planning									
	9,5	discuss,specific plans/proc,									
	9,6	measurement									
	9,7	recording									
	9,8	raising questions (for inv,)									
	9,9	critical reflection									

Figure 4.4   *Coding in SPOC category 9*

during one time interval, then 1 was coded and not 2. Consider the example shown in Figure 4.4. Here, the target pupil was actively involved in discussion about observations and measurement, and an audience to discussion about recording. Of these observations, the teacher was involved only in the discussion about measurement.

The rationale for using the eight process skills of category 9 is presented in Chapter 2. However, because of the great importance attached to category 9, the definitions are presented here in more detail:

9.1 Discussing observations This section refers to a description of characteristics of objects or situations which children have directly perceived through their senses. It may involve comparisons between objects or events, such as similarities and differences. It includes descriptions of the order in which events took place, and descriptions of observations in which a pattern exists ('the biggest went the furthest, then the next biggest and the smallest went the smallest distance'), as opposed to a description of the pattern ('the bigger they are the further they go').

Example. Pupil: 'When you push the blocks down they all float back up.'
        Teacher: 'Does everyone agree with that . . . when you push them down they all float back up?'
        Pupil: 'Yes.'

9.2 Interpretation This section refers to drawing a conclusion or inference for which there is some (though not necessarily sufficient) evidence in the children's findings. It refers to identifying a pattern linking observations or data, and interpolating or extrapolating from observed data whether or not the pattern which justifies it is stated.

Example. Teacher: 'Here's a graph showing how fast the soluble aspirin dissolved at different temperatures. Tell me then, what is the connection between the temperature of the water and the time for the aspirin to dissolve?'
        Pupil: 'As the water gets hotter, the aspirin dissolves quicker.'

9.3 Hypothesizing This section refers to suggesting an explanation for an event, pattern or finding. It must be more than giving a name ('it's condensation'), possibly taking the form of an associated factor ('it's something to do with air'), or a suggested mechanism ('it's because the air gets cold on the side of the can'). It is different from interpretation in that conceptually-based reasons are proposed to account for what is observed. Further evidence is likely to be necessary to test the suggested explanation.

Example: Teacher: 'Now why is D the best floater?'
           Pupil 1:   'Got more air in it.'
           Pupil 2:   'Got more air.'
           Pupil 3:   '. . . air bubbles.'
           (Pupil 1 takes block D out of the water and looks more closely at it.)
           Pupil 2:   'It's lighter.'

Sections 9.4 and 9.5 were originally both about planning – general planning and specific planning. In practice, the observers found it difficult to discriminate between the two and therefore the categories were combined into 9.4 and called Planning.

9.4 Planning This section is concerned with both the general design of the plan (what it is about, what is to be changed, and how any result of that change will be observed), and with discussing specific plans and procedures concerned with carrying out a general plan (how much of this, where does that start from, etc.). This section includes deciding what quantities to use and what to measure and how results are to be observed and measured, but discussion of the measuring process or of the measurements taken are included in 9.6: here the concern is with deciding how they are to be taken.

Example. Teacher: 'How will you be able to tell which slope is the best one for the car to run down?'
           Pupil 1:   'We will measure how far each car travels.'
           Pupil 2:   'Yes, but we'll need to make sure the cars all start from the same place, won't we?'
           Teacher: 'That sounds fine to me. Let me see your results when you have done the test.'

9.6 Measurements This section refers to the discussion of the process of some form of measuring while it is taking place, the description of how it was carried out, and the discussion of the measurements subsequently.

Example 1. Pupil: 'It is 7 cm long.'
Example 2. Pupil: 'The measure is in millimetres.'
Example 3. Pupil: 'Make sure the tape measure is at the end of the line.'

9.7 Recording This range refers to discussion about writing notes, taking down results, or drawing either during a practical activity, or afterwards. It also refers to children talking about the form of record they are making or have made of results.

Example. Pupil 1: 'Put the title at the top.'
       Pupil 2: 'Yes, and write down the measurement. It was 7 cm.'
       Pupil 1: 'The graph is too small.'

9.8 Raising questions This section refers to questions about the subject or content of the activity. It refers to questions which request information, suggest enquiring further, or to challenge statements. It is important that this section is not to be confused with hypotheses expressed as questions.

Example. Teacher: 'Are there any other things you would like to find out about balloons?'
       Pupil: 'Yes, I wonder if red ones fly higher than blue ones.'

9.9 Critical reflection (of procedures) This section refers to discussion, usually at the end of an investigation, of different approaches or procedures that could have been used, and discussion about whether and how alternative procedures or changes in those used would have improved the investigation or achieved a better result.

Example. Teacher: 'Is there any way you could make your test better if you did it again?'
       Pupil: 'Well, I could use a different number of turns.'
       Teacher: 'Would that make it better?'
       Pupil: 'Not really,'
       Teacher: 'Do you think you could improve the investigation (of food choice by snails)?'
       Pupil: 'If we crushed up the cornflakes it would have been easier to make sure there was the same amount as the other foods. And it would have been fairer.'

Other Pupil Talk (category 10)

This category was coded in a similar way to category 9, i.e. 1 for active involvement of the target, 2 for audience involvement, and T for teacher involvement. 'Other pupil talk' contains sections relating to recall of previous learning (10.1), recapping of work done (10.2), reading or discussion of instructions (10.3), discussion about meaning of words (10.4), asking for help from either another pupil or the teacher (10.5), and discussion about organizing the task. For example, consider the following scenario:

Five groups of four pupils have been conducting an experiment to test which paper towel is 'best'. The pupils were required to plan their own test, deciding on which variables to control. After fifteen minutes of the lesson's progress, the teacher went from group to group to assess the progress of the experiments and to give help or hints where needed.

Teacher: 'Tell me what you have been doing.'

Pupil: 'We've been testing three different makes of towels – these three here. Mary is doing the wiping so that the wipes are all the same.'

Teacher: 'Why must you do that?'

Pupil: 'Because it wouldn't be fair to each towel if one was wiped harder than another one was.'

Teacher: 'How are you going to tell which towel is the best?'

Pupil: 'We take 'best' to be the number of wipes needed to clear the table. The best will need the least number of wipes. John judges when the table is clean.'

Figure 4.5 shows the relevant codings for the scenario presented above. Sections 8, 9 and 10 do, therefore, give detailed information about the activities and talk experienced by the target pupil either by being involved directly, or by experiencing the category through the discussion of other pupils or the teacher.

10.OTHER PUPIL TALK	10.1 recall of previous learning
	10.2 recap of work done
	10.3 read out/discuss.instruction
	10.4 about meaning of words
	10.5 asking for help
	10.6 organising task
	10.7 non-task

Figure 4.5   *Coding in SPOC category 10*

Teacher Talk and Activity (categories 11 and 12)

The final two categories, teacher talk (category 11) and non-talk teacher activity (category 12) describe the teacher's involvement with the target pupil, i.e. giving information about the task (11.1) or instructions for carrying out the task (11.2), giving feedback (11.3), or non-task such as listening (12.3), demonstrating (12.2), collating ideas (12.1) or correcting work (12.4). These two categories are coded as a tick or left blank as with section 8.

Example 1. Teacher: 'The name of the force which is slowing down the cars is friction.'

Example 2. Teacher: 'So divide your page into two and on the left-hand side say what is the same, and on the right-hand side list all the things which are different.'

Example 3. Teacher: 'I'm very pleased with your work. You have kept to the task but you did carry the experiments further on . . .'

Example 4. Teacher: 'Stop it Wayne, get on with your work.'

The SPOC provides a picture of the science activities and talk which takes place and is experienced by a target pupil. However, in an earlier chapter the possibility was suggested that the content and context of a task may affect the subsequent behaviour of pupils. The STAR project could not ignore these possible effects, and with the advent of the National Curriculum Attainment Targets this information became even more prominent in the analysis. Therefore, in order to obtain as clear a picture as possible of the activities undertaken by the pupils, information describing the task content was collected on a 'SPOC daysheet'.

THE SPOC DAYSHEET

The daysheet recorded, for each target pupil, a list of resources used for the task being undertaken during the observation intervals, for example, a work card, or outside visit, and a worksheet was attached to the daysheet where appropriate. The equipment used for the task was also noted, for example, yoghurt pots, fishing nets, or wooden blocks. A brief description of the target pupil's task was provided by the observer, and finally an outline of the lesson was described to give information about the organization of the class and the running of the lesson, e.g. 'teacher demonstrated how to count pulse rates to whole class; instructed pupils to work in pairs to investigate effect of physical exercise on pulse rate; teacher collated results on blackboard in form of bar graph and children copied this into exercise books'. A copy of the SPOC daysheet can be found in the Appendix.

THE USE OF SPOC

The STAR observer visited the class for observation twice during the autumn term and twice during the spring term at times prearranged with the class teacher. The teachers were not informed of the identity of the target pupils. This anonymity of the observed pupils was considered to be important in the design of the investigation, as previous research has shown that teachers, albeit subconsciously, tend to pay special attention to those pupils who they know are being observed. The observations were carried out by team members of the STAR project and also by experienced teachers on secondment from their local education authorities. With such a complex looking research instrument such as SPOC, it will be obvious to the reader that some intensive training is required to achieve any reasonable levels of reliability of the observation results. All observers received, therefore, a thorough and intensive training at the beginning of the project and before classroom observation began. The training sessions involved practice in observation using video tapes of children working on science activities, and also involved practical sessions in classrooms which were not directly involved in the main study. Both the ORACLE study (Galton *et al.*, 1980), and the PRISMS study (Galton and Patrick, 1990) found that observers tend to relax their powers of observation after a length of time. In order to reduce this possibility, therefore, refresher training sessions took place at intervals throughout the year.

RELIABILITY

The definitions of categories on the SPOC observation instrument were made as tight as possible. However, as discussed elsewhere in this book, there remains an element of subjectivity. When several observers are collecting data, therefore, there is always the possibility that the results are not reliably accurate. To estimate the reliability of SPOC, both video and live reliability were considered necessary. The video reliability facilitates a form of 'autor-user' reliability in which short video excerpts (of twenty seconds duration) were pre-selected on the basis of those which illustrate specific categories from the observation instrument. Live reliability is essential to determine whether similar pictures of events in the same classroom are provided by the observers. For the live reliability, pairs of observers went into the same classroom and, using synchronized timing, observed and coded the same pupils. From this it was possible to calculate the degree of inter-observer agreement by comparing the paired coding for each individual two-minute interval. Reliability was also checked by use of video, so that several observers coded the same time intervals.

Both forms of reliability were calculated using the Czekanowski–Dice coefficient. The chief advantage of this coefficient is that it gives a measure of percentage agreement for the categories that have been used where an unspecified number may be used to code events, and it ignores the categories remained unused in any episode. As might be expected, the resulting reliability figure for the categories associated with organization were very high (0.97). There is little room for error in deciding whether a pupil is sitting with two or more pupils of the same or opposite sex. The reliability of the process skills, category 9 was our main concern. Overall, section 9 produced a high reliability, achieving 0.7 on the video reliability and 0.9 on the live reliability. A video camera produces only a narrow field of classroom behaviour, and at times a certain amount of guesswork about who is speaking takes place. Given that video excerpts are less satisfactory than live sessions, then, the reliability figures were considered to be of satisfactory accuracy for the purpose of the project.

The present chapter has presented a description of the observation instrument used for research purposes in the STAR project. The following chapter presents some results from use of the SPOC instrument, while Chapter 6 describes how classroom teachers adapted the method of observation for their own purpose of assessing science in the classroom.

5

Science Process Skills in the Classroom – the Observation Results

INTRODUCTION

Systematic observation in the STAR project was employed in two separate ways. First, the SPOC system of observation categories was devised as a research tool, to collect information on children's use of science process skills in their interactive talk and behaviour in the classroom during science activities. Second, SPOC was used and adapted by primary teachers to assess science teaching and learning and to provide feedback on the effectiveness of a lesson in their own as well as a colleague's classroom. The present chapter is concerned with the information gained by SPOC as a research tool. This chapter presents some results from the three years of the project.

In year one of the project, data was collected to provide a description of the science that was being taught in the classroom and the range of science talk used by the children. These were classes of teachers who were 'naive' in the sense that there had been no intervention by the STAR team to raise their awareness of science process skill teaching. The results of year two provide some insight into the effect of the raising awareness of science process skills and knowledge of the general results found from year one's observation. Year three provides information on a new set of teachers who, from the start of their involvement with the project, received feedback and support from their colleague STAR teacher, and from the STAR team.

YEAR ONE OF THE STUDY

During the first year of the STAR project, classrooms were observed using SPOC for four science sessions spread over the autumn and spring terms. Six pupils, called TARGET pupils, were the focus of the observation within each classroom. These

TARGET pupils, two boys and two girls from each of the three achievement bands low, medium and high, as designated by the teacher, were observed for a total of sixteen two-minute intervals. This produced a total of over 4000 observations of children while they were engaged in science in the STAR classrooms.

Pupil talk would be greatly affected by the number of children with whom they are in close proximity. It is more difficult to talk, whether about science or non-task talk, if the pupil is alone than if the pupil is seated in a group of several pupils. The seating arrangements of pupils observed were:

Alone	5%
Same sex pair	15%
Mixed sex pair	1%
Same sex group	21%
Mixed sex group	49%
Whole class	9%
	100%

The majority of pupils were seated with other pupils, either as a group member or as one of a pair of same sex pupils. The opportunity for interactive talk was not, therefore, inhibited by the seating arrangement of the classroom.

TEACHER INVOLVEMENT

Table 5.1 shows the percentage of two-minute intervals in which pupils were engaged in science talk either without the teacher involvement (pupil column), or with the teacher's involvement. These figures are based on data for all age groups and all four observed visits. The total column clearly shows that observations, planning, organizing task and non-task are by far the most regular topics of the conversation. While the non-task level may seem high, the observers reported that the talk was a series of short spurts of conversation rather than sustained periods of off-task talk. Infrequently used skills include hypothesizing, raising questions and critical reflection. When the column of figures showing teacher involvement is scrutinized, one sees that the most regular observed skills were observations and planning, the same two skills as for pupil talk without the teacher involvement, with the addition of recap of work done. One gets a picture, therefore, of the teacher visiting the pupils and asking what they have done and how they have got on with it. The pupils respond by talking about their observations and planning. While one would not expect all levels of skills to be equal, after all one cannot interpret until there is some data from observations on which to interpret, the question posed to the teachers was whether the time spent on teacher intervention would be better spent on encouraging the raising of questions, critical reflecting, and hypothesizing, rather than on observations and planning which pupils tend to talk about even when the teacher is not present. It will be shown later in this chapter that the results of year two of the project reflect on the success of strategies used by teachers to improve on levels of process skills.

Table 5.1 *Frequencies of observed talk by pupils and by pupils with the teacher involved*

	Pupil	Teacher involved	Total
Discussing observations	23.5	10.0	33.5
Interpretation	4.6	4.0	8.6
Hypothesizing	2.9	2.5	5.4
General planning	20.5	9.2	29.7
Measuring	8.5	4.8	13.3
Recording	8.9	1.9	10.8
Raising questions	2.1	3.4	5.5
Critical reflection	1.9	1.0	2.9
Recall of previous learning	1.0	3.5	4.5
Recap of work done	3.5	4.5	8.0
Read out/discuss instruction	3.0	1.4	4.4
About meaning of words	0	1.8	1.8
Asking for help	5.9	2.9	8.8
Organizing task	20.2	0.8	21.0
Non-task	31.1	1.2	32.3

The results of observations in the eight science process skills are summarized below:

Observing The majority of the children engaged in discussion of observations at some time, and over half the pupils did so frequently. This was independent of achievement band. The teacher was also involved in this discussion for a considerable amount of the time.

Interpreting Very little discussion of interpretations was observed. The teacher's involvement in those discussions which did occur was prominent.

Hypothesizing Hypothesizing occurred in less than one in ten of the observations, but again the teacher was prominent where it was observed.

Planning More than three quarters of the children engaged in discussion of planning at some time, and this was observed in 30 per cent of the two-minute intervals. Teacher involvement was relatively great. There were no consistent differences between ages or achievement bands.

Measuring Approximately 10 per cent of the observed intervals included some discussion of measuring. Teacher involvement did not feature highly in these discussions.

Recording In one out of ten of the observation intervals, children were observed discussing recording. The teacher was involved in those discussions on one-fifth of occasions.

Raising questions About fifty per cent of all pupils were observed raising questions for investigation on at least one occasion. Teacher involvement in this area was relatively high. Raising questions was observed in less than 10 per cent of the observation intervals.

Critical reflection Very little discussion of critical reflection was observed (less than 5 per cent of observation intervals).

The SPOC results, therefore, raised some interesting issues concerning the degree of teacher involvement, and the frequency of pupil involvement in an activity. Those process skills which were observed to occur very infrequently were often associated with a high degree of teacher involvement, but so, too, were the very frequently occurring process skills. How important a factor is teacher involvement? Could teacher involvement be differently, perhaps more effectively, allocated? The interesting year two results will show whether teachers were able to modify the degree of pupil activity in the various skills, through various means.

GENDER DIFFERENCES

If teacher intervention is important in the development of science process skills,

Table 5.2   *Observed science processes used by girls and boys both with and without teacher involvement*

	Pupil		Teacher involved		Total	
	Boys	Girls	Boys	Girls	Boys	Girls
Observation	24.9	22.1	10.0	10.1	34.9	32.2
Interpretation	4.4	4.8	4.3	3.8	8.7	8.6
Hypothesizing	3.2	2.6	2.3	2.8	5.5	5.4
Planning	19.9	21.1	10.1	8.4	30.0	29.5
Measuring	7.9	9.0	2.1	7.6	10.0	16.6
Recording	9.5	8.4	2.0	1.8	11.5	10.2
Raising questions	2.2	2.1	3.7	3.1	5.9	5.2
Critical reflection	1.8	2.0	0.9	1.1	2.7	3.1

then it is important to ascertain, before we go any further, whether there is a difference between boys and girls in the level of intervention for different skills. Much research has described girls as lacking in independent thought and having a low level of self-confidence in scientific subjects, while boys lack attention to detail and have a false sense of high self-esteem. One might predict, therefore, that girls would be good at skills requiring great detail and accuracy, but needing help in raising questions, whereas boys would be good at raising questions and hypothesizing.

Table 5.2 shows the level of discussion on the eight science process skills by boys and girls, both with and without teacher intervention. The levels of talk in the eight process skills was similar for boys and girls with the exception of measuring. Girls talked more in this area of skill, but the intervention of the teacher was prominent. Gender did not, therefore, appear to have any great effect on the amount of intervention of the teacher, or on the level of talk in the eight process skills.

PATTERN OF THE LESSON

In one observation session, each pupil was observed for four two-minute intervals, two in the first half of the lesson, and two in the second half of the lesson. If the teacher is required to modify the degree of pupil activity in any of the skills, then he or she needs to be aware of the pattern of a lesson in terms of when the skills tend to be employed. Table 5.3 shows the use of SPOC skills during the early and later parts of the science session for comparison, i.e. it compares the first two observation intervals with the final two. The significant results show that the early part of the lesson is associated with discussion of observations, planning, raising questions, recall of previous learning, discussion of instructions, meaning of words, asking for help and organizing the task. Only two categories tended to occur more in the second half of the lesson – interpretation and non-task talk – and these failed to reach statistical significance. All other categories occurred both in the first and second part of the lesson fairly equally, i.e. hypothesizing, measuring (though slightly more in the first half), recording, critical reflection, and recap of work done. In order to see how these results reflect what goes on in the classroom, consider the following observer's description of one particular lesson:

The investigation To test which make of paper towel mops up the best.

Materials Tomato Sauce, various paper towels, stop watch, cloths, water.

Organization The pupils were put into groups of four. Ten minutes was designated as planning time; materials provided on each table. Each pupil had to have an assigned role, as designated by the group as a whole.

Observations One girl became the dominant leader who issued instructions. She did, however, attempt to allow the whole group to agree with her. A poor writer was assigned the task of recorder. This caused some difficulties as no one could read her writing. She was told what to put down, but other members of the

Table 5.3   *Use of SPOC skills during early and later parts of science sessions*

	Ties	More early	More later	z	2 tail probability
Discussing observations	111	109	82	−1.97	.05 x
Interpretation	211	34	57	−1.84	.07
Hypothesizing	243	33	26	−1.19	.24
Planning	128	131	43	−7.08	.00 xxx
Measuring	203	57	42	−1.48	.14
Recording	198	48	56	− .68	.50
Raising questions	240	38	24	−2.05	.04 x
Critical reflection	268	18	16	− .29	.77
Recall of previous learning	209	73	20	−5.46	.00 xxx
Recap of work done	181	60	61	− .27	.79
Discussing instructions	221	62	19	−4.50	.00 xxx
Meaning of words	256	31	15	−2.14	.03 x
Asking for help	230	45	27	−2.40	.02 x
Organizing task	157	109	36	−5.96	.00 xxx
Non-task talk	193	45	64	−1.81	.07

All pupils: comparison of Round 1 with Round 4 using Wilcoxon signed ranks based on SPOC data aggregated to rounds.

group became frustrated and tried to take over her role while also keeping their own.

A plan was sketched out – one dollop of tomato sauce to be placed on the table. One person assigned to the role of mopper up in order to make the test fair ('we might not wipe the same strength'). The number of wipes needed to clean the sauce from the table was counted by a group member, judged clean by another member, and then recorded. After the first trial, there was discussion concerning the controls used. The decision was taken to have two judges on whether the table was clean. Further discussion and hypothesizing led to modification of the experiment by testing with the towel dry and then wet. The teacher arrived and asked for a recap of what they had been doing. 'What are your controls?'; 'How are you comparing your results?'; 'Do you think one person can wipe the same every time?'. The group were allowed to continue and completed their experiment. Finding that the recording was haphazard, the leader of the group took charge of the whole investigation and took over the recording by remembering what the counts were. She did not seek the help of any of the other members of the group. The other group members, at this point, started to go off-task and be non-involved until the time came to interpret the results in terms of which towel was the better one. The wet Fiesta towel was best, was the final decision. A plenary session then began. All groups described what they had done and then presented their records. Each group was then given time to look at each others records and to comment, to the teacher and other pupils, on the effectiveness of the records and whether the information given in them was good or adequate or poor. All pupils were then invited to offer criticisms of methods used by any of the groups, but also to offer possible improvements. 'Why do you think that towel wiped up the best?' was the next question by the teacher. 'We shall have to come up with some ideas and test them out next time'.

It is easy to see that recording and critical reflection played an ongoing role in the investigation. The experiment was planned, but then modified after critical reflection and raising of questions. Interpretation of the results was not possible until enough data had been collected to look for a pattern or result, and therefore could not happen before the second half of the lesson. Non-task talk began when members of the group became frustrated and unable to participate usefully as a group member. The dominant girl took over and was allowed to do so.

TEACHER DEVELOPMENT

The results from year one observations were presented to the STAR teachers at a conference at the end of the year. These results, together with results from written tests (the Walled Garden), and practical tests (the Sprinkler), were used to encourage teachers to look at their own teaching situation, and to think of possible reasons for the results; to consider how far their own classroom fit the results; and to consider what strategies they might employ for improving science process skills in their own classroom. Teachers were requested to select two process skills and work at improving those in their own classroom, and to share the strategies tried, whether successful or not, with other teachers from the project so that methods could be tried in several different classrooms.

At the conference, teachers participated in a circus of activities which were designed to raise their awareness of science process skills. For many of the teachers the aspect of process skills was totally new to them and they needed to know what was actually meant by hypothesizing, interpreting, etc. before they could begin to consider ways of improving them in their classroom. This circus of activities is discussed in Chapter 6.

SUGGESTIONS FOR ENCOURAGING CHILDREN'S PROCESS SKILLS

At the conference, teachers were encouraged to begin discussing possible strategies for promoting process skills in the classroom. In general, it was considered artificial to attempt to deal with only one or two skills at a time. However, it was agreed that the teacher could have a particular focus in terms of helping the development of one or two chosen skills, while the children are using several of the other skills in their activities.

Several points were made about how teachers might help the development of process skills in general:

- Being aware that you want to develop a specific skill; referring to a list of skills to help to define it; clarifying such goals to oneself and to other teachers.
- Developing the process skills through activities in other areas of the curriculum.
- Allowing time for discussion; gearing language to the ability level of the children.
- Asking productive questions.
- Establishing groups for working; assigning specific tasks within the group but rotating the tasks; arranging for groups to report to groups.
- Introducing and pursuing topics attractive to the children.
- Establishing a school-wide policy for developing process skills.

Teachers considered the development of process skills by taking them one by one. The suggestions are listed below:

Observation Two possibilities for encouraging observation were debated. First, observation could be encouraged within the context of normal activities; second, observation could be made the focus of specially-devised activities. Examples are:

- Use of senses; emphasis on all senses; sometimes focus on one sense.
- Asking for similarities and differences; encouraging comparison; replication.
- Drawing attention to things; pointing them out.
- Observing events; before and after.
- Providing a 'fun' context; a real purpose for observation.
- Use of discussion; productive questions; tabulation of information – similarities and differences
- Encouraging the use of equipment such as hand lenses and microscopes (help from loan services – museums, science centres); build up collections of interesting items.
- Structured questions on workcards or multiple choice sheets about practical activities; supplemented by teacher interaction with responses sometimes tape recorded.
- Circus of experiments around one theme; children report back to rest of class and answer questions.

Interpretation Opportunity for development of interpretation depends essentially on the provision of observations or data for children to interpret. Suggestions included:

- Helping children come up with patterns; giving them a chance and intervening if they do not.
- Using experiences in linked curriculum areas, such as number patterns in maths.

- Providing material for observation suitable for data gathering with a view to graphic representation.
- For top infants – measuring own physical features, drawing simple graphs and looking for trends in class-based work; for top juniors – working in smaller groups with more discussion, more recording.
- Finding their own evidence or using data from a newspaper.

Hypothesizing

- Initiate hypothesizing from practical work rather than from teacher questioning; begin with a very stimulating demonstration.
- Encourage children to think about reasons for unexpected results.
- The teacher might ask questions to which he or she does not know the answer; everyone draws on their experiences to make suggestions for dealing with the problem.
- Ask children to think about 'why' when results are obtained.

Raising questions

- Directing the questioning by giving the children some material and asking 'What do you want to find out?'
- Discussing questions so that children realize which are ones that can be investigated; attempting to help children to rephrase their question to be potentially investigable.
- Brainstorming at the beginning of a topic to find what questions the children have about it; the teacher could start off by raising questions.
- Building up a display of questions, or having a question box or board where questions thought up can be seen.
- Have children in groups, directed so that they need to cooperate and question each other.
- Introduce the context of the activity, then allow a play stage before a plenary to raise questions.

Planning Teachers need to have the confidence to allow children to plan, from an early age, and to realize that workcards often take the opportunity to plan away from children.

- Put the children in situations where they can question and then plan to answer their questions.
- Talk through the planning process so that the children realize what one has to do to plan.
- Use a 'planning board' to highlight the questions to be addressed in planning: What do we want to find out? How are we going to do it? What materials do we need? How do I make the test fair? What measurement or observations do we need? Is the plan safe? What do we record? How do we record?
- Encourage perseverance so that if something goes wrong the children do not give up but learn from what happened; help to see planning as valuable and important.

- Having a planning session the day before the practical session.

Critical reflection

- Children can be encouraged to build modifications into their activities as they go along.
- Give more time for periodic reflection during and at the end of a session.
- Provide opportunities for children to report to each other on their progress; start by encouraging children always to react positively to others' work, to pick out good ideas as well as suggesting ways of improving procedures.
- Encourage children to question each other so that reflection is prompted.
- Report half way through the lesson asking pertinent questions, e.g. Is your test fair? How do you know?
- Ask children to think of two ways to do something. Discuss and improve own efforts – modify.

Recording To encourage effective verbal communication. Models, tables, demos, written, drawings, tapes, graphs, cross-curricular nature.

- Give pupils an audience and then they have to select the best way of recording to present information to that particular audience – recording for a purpose.
- Have a planning board. Critically reflect on each group of children's efforts at the end of the session.

Measurement

- Measuring for a purpose; have measuring as a title on a planning sheet.

These are just some of the strategies suggested by the teachers following group discussion. Year two was to see the use of some of these strategies and the discussion, at several teacher meetings, as to what worked and what did not.

YEAR TWO RESULTS

During the second year of the project, teachers developed their strategies with the help of feedback from observations made by the STAR team. This observation continued as for the first year of the project. The main question at this stage of the project was whether there would be a change in the pattern of interactive talk across the eight science process skills.

The age range of the pupils who were involved in this second year of the project was rather different from that of year one. This age difference was due to teachers changing the age range they taught. As most of the teachers had started the project teaching older juniors, it was inevitable that the change was to younger age pupils. When the general results of SPOC observations were examined, little difference was found between the two years. This lack of increased performance, as one would have hoped for following a year of intervention, is most likely to be due to the younger age range of the pupils in this second year of the project. When the results are compared for fourth year pupils only, the results are more encouraging.

The following results are based on those for fourth year pupils only, although a reduced number in consequence, so that the figures are comparable to those of year one.

The general results for the process skills are presented separately below:

Observing The majority of pupils talked about observation at least once over the sixteen observed intervals. Achievement Level was significant with high achievers talking about observation more regularly than low achievers.

Interpretation Fairly low levels of talk about interpretation of data. Higher achievers talked more than low achievers about interpretation.

Hypothesizing Less than 40 per cent of all pupils were heard hypothesizing. Little difference was found between achievement levels.

Planning Nearly all pupils were engaged in discussion about planning at least once.

Measurement Over half of the children talked about measurement, but less so for the low achievers.

Recording About one-half of all pupils were heard to discuss recording at least once.

Raising questions Less than 40 per cent of all pupils were observed to raise questions. Achievement was not reflected in the results.

Critical reflection Fairly low levels of critical reflection were observed, but the levels showed a marked increase on the levels of year one.

Table 5.4 compares the results of fourth year pupil observations in year one and in year two of the project. When a comparison is made between year one (with no intervention, only normal progression) and year two results (with intervention and following the awareness programme), some differences are noticeable.

The regularity of pupil talk about observation and planning remained at very similar levels over the two years. However, hypothesizing increased from 6.7 to 8.3 per cent, raising questions increased from 4.0 to 6.5 per cent, and critical reflection increased from 2.0 to 7.3 per cent. If there is an increase in some skills, then this has to be at the expense of others. In this case, the levels of interpretation decreased from 9.7 to 7.1 per cent, measurement from 11.7 to 10.3 per cent and recording from 12.3 to 10.8 per cent. While measurement and recording could afford to reduce in regularity, interpretation is more of a concern but may reflect the decrease in data which children gathered because of less measurement and recording. What is apparent is the increase in teacher involvement in the talk, and this may reflect a change in teaching style employed for science.

YEAR THREE RESULTS

In year three of the project, the STAR teachers were encouraged to develop their own observation skills in the classroom, both their own and a colleague's. Further details of this observation is presented in Chapter 6. Here, we are concerned with

Table 5.4   *Results from year 1 SPOC observation compared with year two SPOC observation of science process skills*

	Pupil	Teacher involved	Total
Results from year one (fourth year pupils only)			
Observation	22.0	7.3	29.3
Interpretation	5.7	4.0	9.7
Hypothesizing	3.7	3.0	6.7
Planning	21.0	9.0	30.0
Measurement	10.0	1.7	11.7
Recording	10.0	2.3	12.3
Raising questions	2.0	2.0	4.0
Critical reflection	1.3	0.7	2.0
Results from year two			
Observation	21.5	9.5	31.0
Interpretation	3.9	3.2	7.1
Hypothesizing	5.0	3.3	8.3
Planning	22.6	12.2	34.8
Measurement	8.1	2.2	10.3
Recording	8.6	2.2	10.8
Raising questions	3.2	3.3	6.5
Critical reflection	4.5	2.8	7.3

(The results are presented as a percentage of observed intervals of two minutes duration.)

the effectiveness of the STAR teachers at working with a colleague to improve the levels of science process skills in the classroom.

Six target pupils were observed in the colleague's (known as the 'B' teacher's) classroom at the beginning of the year and again towards the end. Table 5.5 presents the results from year three observations. The regularity of talk in each of the skill categories is very similar to the results of year two of the STAR teachers classrooms. There was slightly less planning and more measurement with less raising questions.

Table 5.5 *Results of SPOC observation in year three of the study*

	Pupil	Teacher involved	Total
Observation	20.0	9.6	29.6
Interpretation	3.5	3.4	6.9
Hypothesizing	4.5	2.8	7.3
Planning	20.5	8.9	29.4
Measurement	10.8	2.0	12.8
Recording	8.6	2.4	11.0
Raising questions	2.6	2.3	4.9
Critical reflection	4.6	2.7	7.3

(The results are presented as percentages of two minute intervals.)

The main interest of the project was whether the collaboration of two teachers in the development of science was successful. If it was successful, then one would expect an improvement in science process skills from the first to the second observation of the 'B' teachers' pupils. This improvement could be measured by comparison with the normal progress one would get in a classroom as measured by the observations of the STAR teachers in the first year of the project.

Table 5.6 presents the results to compare pupil progress when no intervention had taken place, with pupil progress when intervention had taken place.

With the STAR teachers, the skill of observation had levels of 34.7 and 32.2 per cent for the beginning and end of the year respectively, hypothesizing was 6.5 and 6.2 per cent, and planning was 39.7 and 38.8 per cent. These levels were, therefore, similar throughout the year. The levels of recording (4.8 and 8.5 per cent) and raising questions (2.5 and 3.9 per cent) increased at the expense of interpretation (11.6 and 5.6 per cent), measurement (10.7 and 9.3 per cent) and critical reflection (9.4 and 6.1 per cent). Bearing in mind that the purpose of the year was for STAR teachers to work with 'B' teachers to improve the quality of science experience in the classroom by sharing experiences gained, it is encouraging to find that the increases were in areas of concern, as identified from year one observation, and that the increases were at the expense of observation, and measurement; both of which could afford to drop in regularity.

PUPIL PROFILES

At the end of year two of the project, STAR teachers attended a conference to prepare them for working with a colleague and also to develop an observation

Table 5.6   *Comparison of the effect of collaboration between teachers on the development of science process skills*

	Pupil	Teacher involved	Total
Results from year one first observation visit			
Observation	21.9	12.8	34.7
Interpretation	5.8	5.8	11.6
Hypothesizing	3.1	3.4	6.5
Planning	25.4	14.3	39.7
Measurement	8.4	2.3	10.7
Recording	2.2	2.6	4.8
Raising questions	1.3	1.2	2.5
Critical reflection	3.1	6.3	9.4

	Pupil	Teacher involved	Total
Results from year one final observation visit			
Observation	23.4	8.8	32.2
Interpretation	3.3	2.3	5.6
Hypothesizing	4.3	1.9	6.2
Planning	28.1	10.7	38.8
Measurement	7.6	1.7	9.3
Recording	2.7	5.8	8.5
Raising questions	2.1	1.8	3.9
Critical reflection	2.3	3.8	6.1

(The results expressed as a percentage of two-minute intervals.)

scheme. Part of the value of observation was demonstrated by presentation of pupil profiles based on the research observation obtained during the year.

Table 5.7 shows a typical profile of observed pupil talk in science. Pupils are coded 01 to 06 to preserve anonymity. Each pupil was observed for sixteen two-minute intervals and the number of intervals in which each pupil was heard to use one of the science process skills is shown. For example, if the teacher was interested in pupil 01, by looking across the table he or she saw that the pupil displayed very

Results from year three first observation visit		
	Pupil	Teacher involved	Total
Observation	18.3	12.1	30.4
Interpretation	3.5	2.9	6.4
Hypothesizing	3.8	2.8	6.6
Planning	31.8	11.1	42.9
Measurement	9.9	2.0	11.9
Recording	2.2	2.5	4.7
Raising questions	2.6	2.5	5.1
Critical reflection	1.9	2.3	4.2

Results from year three first observation visit		
	Pupil	Teacher involved	Total
Observation	21.7	7.2	28.9
Interpretation	3.5	3.9	7.4
Hypothesizing	5.1	2.9	8.0
Planning	30.8	10.7	41.5
Measurement	7.0	2.8	9.8
Recording	3.0	1.9	4.9
Raising questions	6.6	3.0	9.6
Critical reflection	3.3	2.4	5.7

good levels of talk about observation, scoring 11 out of a possible 16 occasions, and reasonably good levels about measuring, 4 out of 16, but the pupil showed little evidence of his or her skill in interpretation, hypothesizing, planning, and raising questions. No talk took place about recording or critical reflection. The teacher got some idea, then, that the pupil gave evidence of skill in observation and measurement. By looking down the columns instead of across, the range of observation talk is from 1 to 11, whereas for critical reflection the range is only 0

Table 5.7   *SPOC observation profile of science 'talk'*

PUPID	OBSERV	INTERP	HYPOTH	PLAN	MEAS	RECORD	RQNS	CREF
01	11.00	1.00	2.00	2.00	4.00	0.00	1.00	0.00
02	6.00	0.00	2.00	1.00	4.00	0.00	4.00	0.00
03	1.00	0.00	0.00	1.00	1.00	0.00	0.00	0.00
04	4.0	0.00	1.00	2.00	0.00	0.00	2.00	0.00
05	6.00	0.00	1.00	3.00	2.00	3.00	1.00	1.00
06	5.00	0.00	0.00	2.00	1.00	1.00	0.00	1.00

to 1. This may suggest, therefore, that the activity in which the children were engaged was not conducive to talk about critical reflection, i.e. the opportunity for critical reflection was not provided, the reason for which the teacher needs to ascertain. If the opportunity to critically reflect is not provided, then the pupil could not be expected to show evidence of his or her skill in that particular science process. If the teacher feels that the opportunity had been there, then the evidence suggests that none of the pupils had been able to take the opportunity to critically reflect and the learning has not yet been successful. Pupil profiles, therefore, are useful in two ways: first, to provide evidence of what a pupil can do and, second, to aid in evaluation of lesson content.

LESSON CONTENT

The STAR project recognized the importance of lesson content in the influence on children's talk and behaviour. Details concerning lesson content were collected on a Daysheet. This sheet provided a record of the materials and resources used, the content of the lesson, and the organization. Of the lessons observed during the first year of the project, some involved problem solving, some were an investigation, some were mainly practical, some were mainly written, or were a combination of all of these. The frequencies of these types of lessons were:

    18 per cent of activities involved problem solving
    82 per cent involved an investigation
    89 per cent were mainly practical
    11 per cent were mainly written.

The lessons were, then, mainly practical investigations in which written work played a minor role.

    The information relating to the lesson content was coded according to the subject (which would now be attainment targets of the NC). The rank order of incidence of these subjects are shown in Table 5.8.

Table 5.8   *Rank order of incidence of subjects*

Rank	Subject area	% of lessons
1	Movement/forces	21.1
2	Material and their properties	13.7
3	Ourselves and other animals	13.6
4	Water and how things behave in it	13.3
5	Sight, light and colour	9.7
6	Change	6.1
7	Electricity	6.0
8	Hot and cold temperature changes	5.8
9	Air and breathing	5.7
10	Rocks, soil and growth of plants	3.1
11	Hearing and sound	0.7
12	Time – technology	0.1

While the most favoured subjects areas were movement/forces, materials and their properties, ourselves and other animals, and water, the question is posed as to whether any of the subject areas are better at promoting one process skill rather than another. The levels of process skills were greatest in the following subject areas:

Observation:	movement, water, ourselves, material/properties
Interpreting:	movement, water, materials/properties
Hypothesizing:	movement, water, air and breathing
Planning:	movement, materials/properties
Measuring:	movement, ourselves
Recording:	movement, water, materials/properties, sight
Raising questions:	movement, water, sight, materials/properties
Critical reflection:	movement, water, material/properties

As can be seen, nearly all of the process skills were evident in the favoured subjects, with 'ourselves' lending itself to observation and measuring, 'air and breathing' conducive to hypothesizing, and 'sight' conducive to recording and raising questions. Further investigation in this area is necessary, particularly in relation to the National Curriculum attainment targets, but there is the suggestion that some subject areas may be more suitable for development of some process skills than others.

The effect of equipment and resources is another area for further investigation.

Table 5.9 *Equipment and resources used in year one*

Rank	Materials	% of lessons
1	Consumables	56.9
2	Classroom stock	49.2
3	Printed matter	46.5
4	Measuring equipment	38.1
5	Art/craft materials	35.9
6	Scientific apparatus/materials	33.4
7	Miscellaneous	23.8
8	Tools	17.5
9	Domestic equipment	16.6
10	Audio visual aids	8.1
11	Outdoor – visits/grounds	7.2

Do resources affect the curriculum taught, or does the curriculum define the resources to be made available? Do resources change teaching style, i.e. move to practical tasks away from whole class teaching? At the ASE conference in Nottingham, 1988, a speaker from a Bristol junior school suggested that teachers' main obstacles in the teaching of science were a lack of time, lack of confidence, of knowledge, and funds rather than resources. This is a circular problem, however, as a lack of resources could lead to a lack of confidence, but similarly a lack of time even with a strong feeling of confidence would lead to resources not being used. The question to examine, then, is whether the type of resources available affects the type of pupils interactive talk about science.

Table 5.9 is based on the information provided on the STAR daysheets and shows the equipment and resources used in year one.

Consumables come high in the ranking of use in science lessons, while scientific apparatus/materials are used in only one third of the lessons, ranking sixth. Teachers on the STAR project are not, therefore, deterred from teaching science owing to a lack of scientific equipment. What we cannot tell, however, is whether an increase in the use of scientific equipment would lead to improvement in the use of science process skills by the children. This aspect is an area requiring further investigation and will not be covered here.

CONCLUSION

Year one of the project identified some process skills which were rarely in evidence from pupil talk. When these skills did occur, it was usually with the intervention of the teacher. However, the teacher also intervened in skills which were frequently in evidence by the children. The question posed was whether the teacher could improve the science skills of the pupils by modifying his or her intervention role in the classroom.

A raising awareness of what science process skills meant led to teachers improving their science teaching by formulating strategies that were suited to their own classroom situation.

When working with a colleague, the children in the colleague's classroom benefited from the in-service effect of collaborative working between the two teachers. Evidence of children using previously infrequent process skills was provided from the observational study using SPOC.

There are still many areas requiring further investigation, such as the role of the context, and equipment and resources, on the learning process.

Part of the development of teachers was aided by the information provided by observers in the classroom. The provision of an extra pair of eyes in the classroom, while valuable, is expensive and difficult to arrange. The next step, therefore, would be for teachers to observe in their own classroom while also having a teaching role. The following chapter describes how some of the STAR teachers worked towards this role.

6

Observation by Teachers

Publication of observation results from previous research such as Bennett (1976), and ORACLE (Galton *et al.*, 1980) in which an attempt was made to link teaching styles with pupil achievement resulted in a great deal of scepticism and suspect among teachers as to the usefulness and validity of classroom observation. Teachers were heard to express 'I already know my children, I observe all the time', and 'It's in my head, I don't need to write it down', while others recognized the value of observation but questioned, 'How do I find the time?' The first question to overcome with teachers, then, is to justify the need for observation given the numerous demands already being made upon their time. Do they already have the information in their heads?

RAISING AWARENESS

Consider a large audience at a public meeting in a hall. When asked, 'Without looking round, how many of you know where the fire extinguishers are situated?', less than a handful of people are likely to be able to answer in the positive. 'Well,' they might say, 'why should I be able to say where they are, there isn't a need for one – there isn't a fire.' Indeed, there might not be a need at that particular moment, but if a fire should start, then the knowledge of the whereabouts of the extinguishers would suddenly become extremely useful and important. One might conjecture that the audience would spend the following few weeks noticing the position of fire extinguishers in all public buildings they go into simply because they have had their awareness raised. Similarly in the classroom, if teachers only make general observations, the detail which might be important could well go unnoticed. Children interact with the teacher for less than thirty second intervals at a time, and with, say, thirty pupils in a class, the reader is left to calculate the enormity of the total number of interactions in a day. What will the teacher observe from these interactions? Will it be important facts or irrelevancies?

At a recent meeting, teachers were asked to watch a video of children (who were engaged on practical science tasks), and to write down any observations which they felt inclined to make. The results were collated. What did they observe? 'The teacher was working with the children for only ten seconds', 'The children didn't have enough equipment for them all – they had to share' and 'The group were all boys', plus other similar observations. All observations concerned management of the lesson. There was no indication whatsoever of the content of the lesson. It could as easily have been English or RE as science.

Following this observation, the group of teachers participated in a practical session in which they were taken through a circus of activities each designed to raise awareness of one science process skill – in all eight activities for eight science skills. As one example of these activities, which was designed for the participants to work in pairs for a period of about five minutes, a piece of velcro and a magnifying glass were provided and the question posed as to how the two pieces of velcro material 'stuck' together. While the investigation could, if taken far enough, involve all science process skills, the limited time span ensured that only one process skill could be guaranteed to be involved – in this case the making of observations. After this practical session, the teachers then observed the video once more and it was unanimously agreed that far more useful information was gathered from it this second time than before. While a second viewing of the video may have extended the observations even without the skills circus, it would have been likely that the observations would have included more detail on management issues rather than the science content. The teachers had had their awareness raised towards science process skills and as a consequence took notice of the content of the children's behaviour and talk in addition to taking notice of management issues they had observed before. The raising of awareness was the critical element to aid useful gathering of information.

RECORDING OBSERVATIONS

Recent changes in the education system is forcing teachers to produce evidence for the statements they make about pupil achievement. The time has gone when teachers could talk to parents at parents' evenings and rely on informal and unrecorded observations backed up by a few short test results to comment on the progress of their pupils. Some evidence for our assessments can be gathered from written work (Schilling *et al.*, 1990), but the National Curriculum states that a child should be able to 'ask questions and suggest ideas' (Attainment Target 1, Level 2), and 'carry out an investigation with due regard to safety' (Attainment Target 1, Level 4). A child's written responses would be unhelpful in the assessment of these particular items, and others listed in the National Curriculum. We need, therefore, to make observations of the child's behaviour and interactive talk during classroom science activities in order to gather the information required.

Evidence to present to parents is one example of the need for formal observation.

In addition to this need, is the importance of records of information to pass on to future teachers of the pupils. The National Curriculum demands a continuous education so that each child will progress and develop according to his or her needs rather than having to repeat work they have done in previous years, or to omit work that teachers have failed to cover. Teachers are often heard to say at the beginning of the academic year, 'I don't know the children so I don't know what they can do – ask me in six weeks time. I spend that time finding out what they can do.' This will no longer be acceptable or, indeed, necessary. Records of children's achievement must be kept and used if a child's education is to be continuous and tailored to their own individual needs.

So far, then, we have established that teachers need their awareness raised of relevant issues for assessment if useful information is to be gathered through observation. We have also established the need for records of observations of pupil talk and behaviour in science sessions. In addition to these two uses, there is the value of the observations in providing feedback to teachers to facilitate evaluations of their lessons. The employment of class profiles, described in Chapter 5, illustrates the usefulness to the teacher of the information gained from close observation of pupils at work in the classroom. However, teachers are individuals who have their own needs – they have preferences for certain styles of teaching, and for classroom organization. They need, therefore, not only to assess pupils according to the demands of the National Curriculum, but also to evaluate their lessons in terms of the impact of the content on the learning which takes place, and the suitability and effectiveness of classroom management and teaching style. The STAR project felt, therefore, that for a method of observation to be used successfully, it had to be designed by the teachers who were to use it. This task was undertaken in year three of the STAR project.

In year three, the teachers who were involved from the start of the study were now aware of the science process skills as related to the National Curriculum Attainment Target 1, and had tried several strategies in their own classroom to improve the pupils' use of these skills. The time had arrived to share their findings with other teachers as well as continuing to develop further themselves. The original plan of the project was for the teachers to work with teachers from neighbouring schools. However, it was clear that working with other teachers would demand a considerable amount of self-confidence which was not yet fully developed in all of these STAR teachers. It was felt prudent, therefore, to arrange for the teacher to work with a colleague in their own school before being asked to work with strangers. The purpose of the year was for the teacher to develop an observation technique to use in his or her own classroom, and also in his or her colleague's classroom, in order to provide feedback on the lessons and share in the development of science.

As stated above, it was desirable for the teachers to design their own observation method if it was to be useful to them. On the other hand, many teachers were still lacking the confidence needed to embark on new ventures with no help at all. Initially, therefore, a basic observation sheet was provided for the teachers to alter and adapt as they wished. This basic record sheet consisted of a sheet of paper

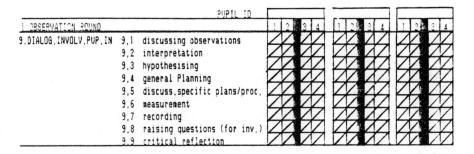

Figure 6.1 *Basic record sheet*

containing at the top a copy of the eight process skills used by the STAR research team, and the rest of the sheet blank (Figure 1). In the initial stages of working with a colleague, it was found useful to concentrate on developing no more than two process skills at a time. While other skills were likely to be involved, they were not to be the main concern of the development of strategies for improving the science in the classroom.

Several adaptations of SPOC resulted from the year's work. Figure 2 shows one example. For this version the teacher had a record sheet for each child observed, and observed children who were working in a group. The dynamics of group work were of particular interest to this teacher who, therefore, wished to record details concerning the size of group, gender and ability mix, and the roles played by each member of the group. A space was provided to record which process skills were the focus of attention for that observation period, and the skills were listed with blank spaces at the side for free notes.

After a session in which a STAR teacher had observed a colleague's lesson, the two teachers discussed together the effect of the lesson. The colleague had his or her own evaluations, but now had the additional help of having had an extra pair of eyes in the classroom. The focus of the lesson would be discussed beforehand so that the observer teacher could base the observations on those aspects of the lesson which were relevant. The following extract is an example of observations noted and recorded by an observer and teacher working together on the development of planning skills.

- The activity allowed for the development of planning skills and these were observed.
- In some groups ideas were not collated or shared. Some children had 'ideas' but these were often ignored or rejected by more able forceful children. Consequently these children lost interest, became passive and took on the role of equipment collector. 'I've been sat here for forty minutes and I've done nothing . . .' (Paul)
- Some groups worked on a trial and error basis. The costing of materials did require some early planning but little time was spent on this. Alternatively, one group of two spent twenty minutes on design and costing. In some cases, the costing of materials became inhibiting and prevented the children the

SPOC

Name _____

Task _____

No. in group	Mix of group	Role in group

Skills focused on

_____

Observing

Interpreting

Hypothesizing

Planning

Measuring

Recording

Raising questions

Critical reflection

_____

Time observed

Childrens comment

Figure 6.2   *Example of SPOC sheet*

opportunity to make things better at the expense of keeping costs down.

- There was little 'testing' of materials used during the investigation.
- The children accepted the 'weights method' as the only means of testing their pier. The finished product was accepted.
- Children deciding purposefully to make something better by replanning (i.e. critical reflection) was rarely recorded.
- Teacher intervention at any stage was minimal. The exception to this was where the teacher gave information at the beginning of the activity.

It is interesting to note the final item of these observations – that teacher intervention was minimal. This demonstrates that time is available here for the class teacher to be able to observe and gather information.

Figure 6.3 shows an adapted mini SPOC sheet in which tick boxes remained at the top for a quick survey of skills involved in the interactions, and the rest of the

		PUPIL ID											
1 OBSERVATION ROUND		1	2	3	4	1	2	3	4	1	2	3	4
9,DIALOG,INVOLV,PUP,IN	9,1 discussing observations												
	9,2 interpretation												
	9,3 hypothesising												
	9,4 general Planning												
	9,5 discuss,specific plans/proc,												
	9,6 measurement												
	9,7 recording												
	9,8 raising questions (for inv,)												
	9,9 critical reflection												

GROUP MEMBERS | TARGETS COMMENTS

OTHER COMMENTS FROM GROUP

GENERAL OBSERVATIONS FROM AROUND YOU

CONCLUSIONS FROM EXERCISE – SUCCESS OR OTHERWISE

Figure 6.3 *Adapted SPOC sheet*

sheet divided into sections to allow free notes, but under specific headings. The teacher was particularly interested in the quality of interactions about the skills and wished, therefore, to record actual comments made where relevant. It is interesting to note that the teacher has provided a section at the bottom of the sheet to allow for thoughts of what he or she has learnt from the information gathered, and considers the way forward in the light of such information. The following extract is an example of teacher observations which followed from the discussion of observer and teacher and resulted in consideration of the way forward from what they had learnt.

Magnets
Equipment and materials: magnets, screws, paper clips etc. given out to each table.

Focus skill: recording

Positive Observations: raising questions, hypothesizing, discussing observations, making observations, planning independently

> The children explored the magnets for approximately one and a half hours! Most were on-task during the whole of this time. Their reactions to discovery was contagious. The number of questions the children were asking rose considerably. Recording in the way the teacher had intended never happened. We both felt it was a pity to stop the action.

> Pupil 1 comments:
> 'So what do we do next if we can't write, talk or draw?'
> 'Hey look its stuck to my braces.'
> 'Does it stick to brass?'
> 'Nope.'
> 'Why not?'
> 'It's a layer of brass and then a layer of something else.'
> 'I wanna see if they'll move on that (wire) sheet.'
> 'Let's see if they pick up.'
> 'What if they're wet?'
> 'They'll sink won't they?'
> 'It won't stick to them because they're brass.'
> 'Let's see, if anything, its stronger underwater . . . It drops the chip when it comes out of the water . . .'

Future strategies/ideas: as an example of learning by discovery the lesson had succeeded. From what the children have learnt by explaining for themselves there is a great starting point for developing the investigative process. Most of the children had explored in a very unstructured way. Many had flitted from one idea to another. Some great observations had not had a chance to develop. We felt it might be interesting to now bring in some structure; introduce 'specific' investigations and gradually work through the stages of the investigative process basing this on the ideas they had got for the explanation session.

Perhaps planning their next investigation might be introduced as a short but

		PUPIL ID										
1.OBSERVATION FORMD			1	2	3	4	1	2	3	4	1	2	3	4

9.DIALOG,INVOLV,PUP,IN 9.1 discussing observations
9.2 interpretation
9.3 hypothesising
9.4 general Planning
9.5 discuss,specific plans/proc,
9.6 measurement
9.7 recording
9.8 raising questions (for inv,)
9.9 critical reflection

Increasing complexity

Similarities and Differences ☐ Using Senses ☐
Observation ☐ Sorting and Classifying ☐ Optical Instruments ☐
Interpretation ☐ Following instructions ☐ applying information ☐
Hypothesising ☐ Predicting ☐ Suggesting ideas ☐
Planning ☐ Fair Testing ☐ Preparing and using apparatus ☐
Measurement ☐ Estimating ☐ Calculating ☐
Recording ☐ Drawing diagrams ☐ Drawing Charts + Graphs ☐
Raising Questions ☐ Persuing own ideas ☐ Research Skills ☐
Critical Reflection ☐ Modifying ☐ Re-testing ☐

Technology skills

Problem Solving ☐ Designing ☐ Making ☐

Attainment Target Categories

1) Variety of Life ○ 5) Types of Materials ○ 11) Information Transfer ○
2) Processes of Life ○ 8) Earth and Atmosphere ○ 12) Energy Transfers ○
3) Genetics and Evolution ○ 9) Forces ○ 16) Sound and music ○ 16) Earth in Space ○
4) Human Influences on Earth ○ 10) Electricity + Magnetism ○ 15) Using Light ○

Concepts

1)
2)
3)
4)

Figure 6.4 Adapted SPOC sheet with detail linked to National Curriculum

specific activity in itself. This might be better done at a different time to the investigation.

Recording: there is a need to get children to share their ideas with others. During the explorative session this didn't really have time to be focused on. It may be that ways of recording might have to be discussed with the children, i.e. getting some of their ideas about how best to record and share with others what they've done. Groups could talk in groups about what they did and results they got – perhaps even present results to another class.

Hypothesizing: getting children to guess why something is happening is something that still needs a teacher's help! We felt that this activity had been a great start which now can gradually and carefully become more structured so that the children become more thoughtful and see the need to plan and record what they have found out.

Figure 4 provides a rather different adaptation of the mini SPOC sheet. Here, the tick boxes remain at the top, but the teacher wished to break each of the eight process skills into more detail, and specifically detail linked to the National Curriculum. The section immediately beneath the tick boxes contains three columns of items. The columns were intended to contain items in increasing complexity as one moved to the left. A section was also provided to include which Attainment Target was involved in the content of the lesson, and a section to list the science concepts involved. This sheet was an initial attempt to bring in the National Curriculum to the STAR project, and was based on the interim report and not the final document. The teacher subsequently developed other records which he felt more useful and suitable for use, but this record is shown here to demonstrate the trials taken by the teacher before coming up with an acceptable form.

TIME

To enable the STAR teachers to work with a colleague and to spend time observing in each others' classrooms, the local authorities supported the teachers by providing financial assistance for supply cover. This support was considered to be vital if each pair of teachers were to be able to share their experiences and develop the confidence to be able to offer in-service help to teachers from other schools. The working together of these teachers is described and discussed in Chapter 7 and will be mentioned only briefly here.

All of the teachers found observation to be extremely valuable and useful. However, it proved to be easier to observe in their colleagues' classrooms than their own for two main reasons. First, the teachers did not have supply cover for observing in their own classroom but were left to develop strategies for making it possible. Second, the teachers reported that it was easier in colleagues' rooms as 'they didn't know the children and therefore could be more objective'. In their own classrooms, they tended to read between the lines and put their own interpretation on what children said or did. In one case, a concern was expressed about 'making wrong judgements'. While this was true when the teachers first started to observe,

the teachers tended to become more confident in their judgements about scien
process skills after several observation sessions and reiteration of the definitions of
the skills. Teachers also became more objective with their own children once
practised in the art of observing with pupils from other classes, although it is
recognized that all assessment contains some element of subjectivity. The important
aspect of assessment is that it must give information that helps the teacher to
provide the right learning situation for the child concerned.

The biggest problem for the teachers to overcome was how to find the
opportunity to observe in their own classroom. This is probably the question all
teachers reading this book will be asking, too. Needless to say, the answer is not
straightforward. Each school, each classroom, has an individual way of working.
Some teachers are in lone mobiles, others team teaching with two or three
colleagues. One of the STAR teachers was adamant that observation was just not
possible in his school situation. It is ironic that the teacher, at the end of the project,
was issuing advice to other teachers on how he managed to do it successfully.

So how can one find time to observe in the classroom when there is not supply
cover? Some methods have already been suggested in Chapter 3 – a closer link
between teacher training institutions and schools to involve students in the
observation process; use of a non-teaching head; and others. But some of the STAR
teachers met the challenge by trying out different strategies for managing the lesson.
One of the STAR groups of teachers recognized that teachers tend to like to be
wanted in the classroom. If children get on by themselves, teachers feel redundant
and this produces a feeling of discordance. The lesson is often managed, therefore,
in such a way that the teacher is constantly in demand or busy with housekeeping
duties. Changing behaviour is difficult – there is no easy path. There is a need to
stand back and look at what is happening in the classroom for the teacher to
question his or her own role. How necessary is the teacher's role at each stage of the
lesson. Would group attention be more efficient without losing effectiveness and
thereby cutting down on the time given to providing instructions and explanations.
Several STAR teachers analysed their way of working to see if time for observation
could be made available. One example will be described in detail. The teacher
identified a period at the beginning of a practical science session during which he
was in constant demand by the pupils. Children demanded his time and attention
often because of their poor planning skills. The children had a poorly-designed
experiment and soon encountered difficulties and subsequently sought help and
advice from the teacher. To overcome this pressure on his time, the teacher first
organized the pupils into manageable groups depending on the maturity of the
children and the previous experience they had. These groups, usually of three or four
pupils, were always mixed boys and girls. These small groups were then set a task
concerned with the early planning stages of an investigation. For example, 'Ask
each other a question about bubbles. Write down your questions.' A time limit was
given for this – a few minutes – and groups then paired up to compare notes. During
this time, the teacher became free to observe group interactions and to identify
where difficulties might arise and thus where his help might be demanded. He was
also, in this case, able to look for evidence of pupils raising questions. This session

by a full class report back session before the practical work
ng has been observed, and discussed, then the practical part of
re less teacher involvement for help and leave the teacher time
y working with groups, listening and questioning to shape the
tigation and subsequent learning of the children.

Another teacher, experienced at observing in other people's classrooms, found it difficult to observe in her own. The pupils were dependent for the most minor things such as asking permission to borrow a rubber or to sharpen a pencil. If children are independent then the teacher has more time to deal with the teaching and assessing of science without the constant interruptions of housekeeping duties.

To sum up, several versions of an observation record were tried, and strategies were employed to enable observation of the teacher's own classroom. When asked at the end of the STAR project which method of observation was preferred, without exception the teachers said, 'free field notes – a blank sheet of paper with me while I am working with a group of children'. However, one teacher added a rider that she only preferred free field notes because she was aware of what she wanted to observe. It was important to identify the focus of the observation and look for it rather than to have no focus at all and observe nothing. The field notes were then all transferred to record sheets after the event. This freedom allowed the teachers to observe while working with a group of children. There was no need for observation to be non-participant. From one teacher's comments one might conjecture that there is a further step in the development of the teacher's observation technique; once a useful record sheet had become established, the free field notes would eventually lead to note taking directly onto the record sheets in order to cut down on the administration required, but that, at the moment, must remain conjecture. Teachers have always gathered information from working with the children, and then keeping it in their heads. This method is the same, but with the addition of actually writing the observations down as a response to the need to gather evidence about several, but well-defined, aspects of the children's learning.

SUMMARY

(1) *Raising awareness* In order to assess children in science, the teacher needs to be aware of what he or she is looking for. Assessing pupils without a focus is unhelpful.
(2) *Evidence* In order to produce evidence for a teacher's assessment of a child, some record must be kept. These same records must be helpful in providing information to future teachers of each child in order to ensure a continuous education. These records must be useful to the teacher who is making them.
(3) *Time* Time for observation may be found in two ways. First, by using other agencies such as teacher training institutions, or by using free teaching time of the headteacher (in schools with non-teaching heads). Second, by analysing the role and workload of the teacher in the lesson with the possibility of adapting the lesson organization or teaching method employed in order to leave the teacher free to take on the role of observer.

7

Change in Teaching Primary Science

This final chapter is about the STAR teachers and their development during the three years of the STAR project. It is based largely on their personal accounts of changes in practice. It begins with a set of quotations from the final evaluation documents written by the teachers from two of the local authorities. After a consideration of the issues raised by these comments, we shall go back to the beginning of the project and retrace the steps and decisions taken along the way which may have had a bearing on these perceived outcomes. In particular, the two STAR conferences and the last year of the project in which each of the original cohort of STAR teachers (the 'old STARs') worked with a colleague (the 'new STARs') will be described. In so doing, this chapter will provide a recapitulation of some of the work reported in the preceding chapters.

PERSONAL PERCEPTIONS OF CHANGE

. . . Yes, I have changed my practice in teaching science. I tend to do *more* of it and make sure that I provide open-ended situations as opposed to telling the children what will happen or how to find the answers. The children enjoy this much more, and I find a benefit that I had not expected – the children become so involved, it leaves more time for me to do other things, observe children, or assess. (1)

I have changed my teaching to give the children more open-ended questions and freedom in setting up apparatus. Working on the same topic (as my STAR teacher) helped to give a different approach as did having someone to discuss ideas with. (2)

My confidence has increased. Yes, my practice has changed. I do not merely present them with a science work-card and the appropriate apparatus. I may ask them for ideas as to how to solve a problem, or as to what apparatus they think appropriate. They are given far more opportunity to think for themselves. (3)

These responses were written by the group of 'new STAR' teachers who joined the project in its third year, to the following questions:

> Since working with your partner teacher, do you feel that you have changed your practice in teaching science? If so, in what ways? Do you feel that your attitude towards teaching science has changed, and in what ways?

During that year, each of the original STAR teachers (the 'old STARs') worked with another teacher in the same school. The LEAs supported this stage by providing supply cover and/or personnel to enable the two teachers in each school to work together.

The 'old STARs' responded independently to a similar set of questions which asked:

> Do you feel that your partner teacher has changed his or her practice in teaching science since working with you? If so, in what ways? Do you feel that his or her attitudes towards teaching science have changed, and in what ways?

The following comments were made by the 'old' STAR colleague of the writer of example (3):

> Yes, (3) admitted to being secondary biased in approach but now appreciated how to work with primary science. Has more confidence and is not so worried about the children making a 'mess'. They are now not so directed in their science but encouraged to think for themselves and the teacher does not intervene so often or dismiss ideas out of hand – the pupils can work through them.   (4)

Another pair responded as follows. The 'new' STAR teacher wrote:

> Have become more used to considering the skills which might be developed from particular science activities. Am increasingly concerned to integrate science within topic work.   (5)

(5)'s STAR partner wrote:

> Yes, (5) has become more aware of the process skills involved and is devising strategies to make sure all the processes are developed – before, mainly concentrated on observation – now more flexible.   (6)

These comments were typical of the teachers' responses. The 'new' STAR teachers and the majority of the 'old' STAR teachers were positive about changes in practice and attitude.

CONFLICTING INDICATIONS OF CHANGE

In spite of the self-perceived changes in practice reported above, the results of the classroom observation reported in earlier chapters suggest some, but relatively little, change detected at this level. It could be, of course, that the teachers *were* using strategies which provided opportunities for change, but that the children would not or could not respond to them. Numerous reasons can be suggested for this.

Whatever the explanation, there appears to be some mismatch between the teachers' perceptions and the observations of pupils' behaviour. The comments written by two of the old STAR teachers might provide some explanatory clues to the paradox: namely, that although the teachers felt that their practice had changed substantially, classroom observation of both the old and new STARs' pupils revealed relatively little change and even a decrease in some skills areas across the whole age range. The first teacher wrote of his colleague:

> Has tried to focus on skills more, but still a bit unsure of how to identify them in the classroom. Attitude *is* changing, but still likes to see a conclusion to the lesson (nothing too wrong with that provided skills are being practised).   (7)

The second teacher had moved to a senior position in a new school and was working with the school's science curriculum leader. She wrote:

> Yes and no. The change was very gradual – we need longer than a year, difficult to impose change when someone has a more established style.'   (8)

These responses raise four issues which will be considered in the following pages. These are: (1) changing attitudes; (2) the time factor; (3) the particular difficulties of working with an expert; and (4) the choice of the phrase 'impose change'.

FACTORS IN CHANGE

Changing Attitudes

These two teachers were faced with situations similar to those facing the STAR team at the beginning of the project in that they were working with experts. The old STARs whose partners were beginner science teachers felt that their partners *had* adopted a process skills approach. Those whose new STAR partners were already experienced in primary science teaching, or who had a strong established style, reported greater resistance to the approach. This resistance was a reiteration of that put up by the old STARs themselves at meetings in the early stages of the project. There were protests that 'good teachers are doing this all the time anyway', although the classroom observations suggested otherwise, or during the second stage that it 'was impossible to identify or focus on particular skills because they were all part of a seamless process'. In some cases, it was not until they began to plan for work with other teachers that they openly endorsed the importance of providing opportunities for children to practise science process skills. In other words, once they began to encourage other teachers to adopt a skills emphasis in their teaching, their attitudes shifted from complacency to advocacy.

Time to Change

The question of attitude change is perhaps essential. It may be that the comments made by the teachers about the change in their practice represent a change in attitude which must precede any externally detectable change in practice. The second teacher quoted above pointed out that change was gradual, 'we need longer than a year'. Perhaps the attempt to detect change at the level of the children's behaviour was over optimistic. The attitude change in the first group of teachers took a year *and* a change in role to become agents of change. This second role demanded a restructuring of their thinking and planning about teaching. To seek external independent indicators of change before this had taken place was perhaps doomed to detect only limited or superficial change. During the third year it was common for the old STARs to comment on the benefits to their own teaching which they had discovered by working with another teacher. Here are a few of the many comments to this effect:

> Found that working in someone else's classroom helped focus my own observation in my own room.   (9)

> Observation of another class – this was helpful to me.   (10)

> Discussion afterwards with X very useful. Made me aware of my own class. (11)

> It has made me and my partner aware of areas we need to modify and develop in our approach. I look forward to observing my own class.   (12)

With hindsight, perhaps the formal STAR observations should have continued to seek change in the practice of the old STARs during this phase thus allowing a two-year span for the detection of change.

Working with an Expert

The teacher who wrote quotation (8) above had the potentially difficult task of working with a science curriculum leader with a well-established style and a post-experience science education qualification. Rather than working on a potentially confrontational, one-to-one basis, the old STAR suggested a collaboration policy in which both STARs worked with the rest of the school's staff. While this policy obviously provided an amicable solution to the 'newcomer–expert' dilemma, it diluted the individual attention possible in a one-to-one partnership.

In another school, an old STAR was to work with a new infant teacher whose recent training had introduced her to science process skills. In this sense, the new STAR was an expert. The old STAR capitalized on this by working cooperatively with the rest of the school. The old STAR, who had pioneered the approach single-handed in her school, relished the existence of an ally and reported better liaison between the infant and junior departments of the school.

Paths of Change – Imposed, Offered or Supported

Quotation (8) raises another issue which was under constant review during the STAR project. The teacher has chosen the phrase 'impose change'. The question of 'imposition' is a fundamental issue of teaching and learning at any level, but particularly when the learners are themselves teachers. In the STAR project, the teachers were asked to introduce opportunities for their children to practise science process skills and the particular skills to be encouraged were indeed 'imposed'. The question remained, however, about finding teaching strategies to encourage the children to use these skills. Three general approaches could have been used. One extreme, already in use in one authority, was to *present* the teachers with a set of what were essentially lesson plans which would ensure opportunities for the practice of particular skills within particular contexts. The effect of this approach on the teachers' attitudes will be discussed below. In the remaining three areas, the dilemma for the project team was whether to *offer* a range of general teaching strategies leaving the teachers to apply them as or when they wished, or whether merely to provide *support* and time for the teachers to devise and test their own. Arguments for both approaches were strong. On the one hand, the *offering* of a variety of teaching strategies would have provided them with some 'raw materials' with which to work. On the other hand, providing support and feedback for the development of individuals' strategies would be more likely to (a) take account of specific situational factors intrinsic to the workings of a particular class, and (b) permit greater ownership and perhaps engender greater commitment.

The *presentation* scheme carries an implication that the teachers need a supply of strategies before they have had the opportunity to produce their own. This could stifle those who did have ideas while fostering dependency in those who did not, or who needed longer to devise their own strategies. If these teachers came to rely on outside support then the establishment of an innovation might depend on continued external support. Effects such as these were clearly discernible when the teachers from all four areas came together to think about working with a partner at the second STAR conference.

The *offering* scheme would present a sort of 'shop window' of teaching strategies, such as those described by Joyce and Weil (1986), which would have a much broader application than the scheme above. The teachers would be exposed to information about different models of teaching; decisions as to when, where and whether to use them would remain with the teachers. The problem here, even so, is that once a new idea is offered, it could still limit personal creativity.

The *support* scheme attempts to overcome this problem by making the assumption that the teachers do have a range of strategies to try as well as the confidence to do so. The difficulty here is that it may take longer for these strategies to be refined or articulated. Thus, the presentation scheme might produce short-term, rigid change whereas the support scheme might produce more gradual, more flexible and more persistent change.

It is interesting that the adviser from the local authority that was already committed to an extreme form of 'presentation' scheme, was the most critical in the final evaluation of the effects of STAR. Teachers from this authority were said to be confused about the aims of the project, in spite of receiving the same information as the others and having the most consistent and dedicated 'STAR agents' throughout the project. By contrast, the teachers of another authority who had been characteristically cool in the early stages prepared a book of strategies and put on a highly successful inset day for forty teachers from all over the authority. In this area, ironically, information about paths of change fell short even of the *offering* model and operated solely on a *support* basis providing in effect a complete 'ownership' model.

Various interpretations of this dilemma will be discernible in the next few pages as we retrace the steps through the project from summer 1986 to summer 1989.

RETRACING THE STEPS OF THE STAR PROJECT

The STAR project provided the opportunity for two large groups of teachers, the old STARs and the new STARs, to adapt their approach and practice of primary science teaching to engage children at least as much in the process of science as in its content; to get children to raise questions, plan and carry out investigations and apply their scientific knowledge to attempt to explain their findings.

The project began with groups of between ten and twelve teachers whose expertise ranged from those who had diplomas in primary science, to those for whom the inclusion of science activities would be a new departure. All of the teachers were prepared at the outset to participate in a three-year project which would involve visits from a classroom observer at least four times a year, and attendance at at least one meeting in school time and one outside school hours each term. This describes the minimum commitment; in most cases much more time was given to STAR. In terms of historical perspective, these commitments were made before the advent of directed time and a National Curriculum which would make science a core subject and which, in the end, would give science process skills the relatively high profile they now possess.

THE FIRST YEAR

The first year was simply a year of data collection: there was no attempt to provide any feedback to individual teachers, but meetings were held to report general findings and to begin to acquaint the teachers with an approach to primary science which was either novel, or a change in emphasis, for beginners and experts alike. Responses ranged from bewilderment in some faces, to utter confidence that the process skills in the model were already well catered for and regularly monitored.

In addition to the individual differences between the teachers, and being aware of the dangers of generalization, there appeared to be regional differences in educational philosophy, as hinted above. In one authority, for example, a programme of science sessions based explicitly on the skills in Wynne Harlen's model had been developed by the advisory teachers following a series of in-service courses. This provided a very clear structure for the teachers in that area. In complete contrast, the prevailing philosophy in another area stoutly rejected any form of structure or challenge to the autonomy of the individual class in discovering and following its own course.

The results of the classroom observation made in the first year revealed that the majority of the children had demonstrated each of the eight process skills through their classroom talk on at least one observed occasion. Less than 10 per cent, however, showed any consistency by using the skills on more than one occasion when being observed.

THE FIRST STAR CONFERENCE

The above findings were presented to the teachers at the first STAR conference. They were important for two reasons: first, they reassured teachers who expressed the view that nine, ten and eleven year olds could not form hypotheses or show higher order skills. The fact that a majority of the children *had* done so showed that the teachers were not being asked to do the impossible. Second, this reduced the challenge for the STAR teachers by showing that there was no need for them to foster the use of process skills from scratch. The task became that of providing sufficient opportunities for the use of these skills to flourish.

A further set of findings related to teacher involvement in the children's use of process skills in their talk. The observations revealed that planning investigations and making observations formed a high proportion of the children's talk in the absence of the teacher. Skills such as hypothesizing and critical reflection on procedures were rarely observed, but when they were, they were more likely to have been provoked by teacher intervention than the other skills.

The first conference had four functions. It brought all the STAR teachers together in one place for the first time. This had an unforeseen positive effect on their attitudes to the project and on their motivation by reducing the comparative isolation felt by some of the teachers. Many of those present remarked with surprise on the number of people involved in the project and became aware of the scale of the project. The second function, as described above, was to report the results of the first year's observations and pupil assessments.

The third function was to acquaint the teachers with the eight process skills in the model. This was done by means of a 'circus' of practical mini-tasks devised by Wynne Harlen at Liverpool. The teachers worked in pairs, each partnering someone from a different LEA. The important feature of this exercise was not the completion of the tasks themselves, but the meta-cognitive task of deciding which process skills were being exercised. The pairs' conclusions formed the basis of discussion groups, each chaired by one of the research team with the aim of defining the skills more clearly in terms of practical tasks. This strategy, and the content of the 'skills circus' were used again and again during the project by teachers in their own schools during the third phase. Towards the end of the third phase, it was developed in two ways, both indicative of the old STARs' development; in one authority, the teachers constructed a similar circus of their own activities, while in another the original activities were modified and added to as part of an in-service day for non-STAR teachers.

The fourth purpose was for the teachers to share and devise strategies for promoting children's use of the skills in their classroom practice. These strategies would form the basis of the action research phase. They were to be evaluated in the classrooms by the teachers themselves and, on four occasions, by using the classroom observer to provide feedback on their effectiveness.

THE SECOND PHASE – ACTION RESEARCH

Two aspects of this phase are worthy of note here. The first concerns the changed role of the classroom observers from pure observer-visitor to that of counsellor-cum-colleague. As in the first year, they made four visits to each teacher between autumn and late spring. Thanks to the support of the LEAs, the same people were, in most cases able to continue to visit the same classes during the second phase and so were able to build on the acquaintances or relationships already formed.

THE OBSERVERS' ROLES

The shift from straight-forward observation to observation followed by discussion was not an easy move in every case. The observer was to respond on a teacher-to-teacher basis in discussing the effectiveness of the strategy in relation to the performance of these children. Thus the observers were not expected to adopt any form of advisory role in the sense of artificially importing or transplanting ideas about content, by demonstrating or even by working alongside. Neither were they expected to evaluate the sessions they observed. A very clear policy was adopted with the intention of supporting and counselling teachers to develop their own ideas and to share them with other teachers. These principles were consistent with the contemporary zeitgeist in classroom observation (e.g. Sheal, 1989; Williams, 1989; Sanger, 1988). They represented an 'acceptable face of classroom observation' with an emphasis on support and teacher development rather than input, evaluation and appraisal.

Some of the teachers had to adjust too: rather than expecting a global judgement about the observed session, they had to practise using the informational content of the observations of the children. Thus principles and expectations did not always match.

COLLECTING EVIDENCE OF PROCESS SKILLS IN ACTION

The second aspect was the way in which the teachers' strategies for the promotion of skills were to be evaluated. Post-observation discussion was to focus on what had actually been observed, with particular attention being paid to the three 'teacher targets' chosen by the teacher as high, middle and low achievers, but perhaps also with particular characteristics which the teacher wanted to monitor.

At local meetings, the teachers discussed the kinds of evidence of a strategy's effectiveness that might be collected in the absence of the STAR observer. One common principle was that two and, if possible, three forms of evidence such as a child's spoken words, his or her use of equipment, attitude to or length of concentration on the task, or perhaps a write-up of the task should be recorded. Alternatively, a strategy could be regarded as successful in fostering the use of a skill if all three 'teacher target' children uttered statements that were identified as exhibiting the focus skill in action.

The recording of this evidence was also discussed, but any hope that the teachers themselves would produce their own method of recording evidence had to be abandoned. The teachers were even then too burdened to start inventing and testing action research records. Eventually, the research team produced a sheet of simple questions about which process skills, what concept area, what teaching strategies would be used, and what form of evidence would be collected to determine whether the skills had been used.

PROGRESS AND PROBLEMS

At that time, a process skills approach to primary science was still novel, although since then the introduction of the National Curriculum has made 'the exploration of science' an important component of the primary curriculum. Many of the teachers were still uncertain about the definition and identification of the particular skills, although a small minority were already looking for differences in the quality of pupil performance within the skills. Thus progress in action research in testing strategies to foster specific skills was limited at this stage, and the original plan for the teachers to prepare workshops for the new cohort of STAR teachers was abandoned. Instead, the research team set up a conference to cover dissemination to the teachers of the second year's results, sharing the strategies developed and tested by means of action research and finally to address the task of working with a colleague.

THE SECOND STAR CONFERENCE

The planning of the second conference again faced the question of whether to introduce new ideas or to develop teachers' own approaches. Once more the latter held sway and techniques to encourage self-evaluation and the sharing of strategies were devised. The first was done by means of 'the flower task', which was suggested by Susan Cavendish. Each teacher was given a large drawing of a climbing rose and was invited to represent three positive and three negative influences on their own progress during the year by means of positive and negative influences on the growth of the rose. Sun, rain and fertilizer might be positive influences used to represent an influx of new science resources, active support from the head teacher and sharing ideas at STAR meetings respectively. Pests, frost and unskilled pruning might be represent limited facilities, a rigid timetable and too many other school duties might be seen as detrimental to growth.

This task was administered under the strict understanding that the resultant 'picture' was for personal use only, and so the teachers' actual characterizations were not collected. Instead, the teachers shared their general reflections with each other in pairs and groups, before moving to the second stage of the overall task which was to share particular strategies devised not only for the promotion of process skills, but also for the deployment of resources, for ways to counteract a rigid timetable and so on. As a continuation of the 'garden theme', which threaded its way through all aspects of the STAR project (see Schilling *et al.*, 1990; Russell and Harlen, 1990) following discussion in cross-LEA groups, the teachers wrote these strategies, tips for their implementation and pointers to potential difficulties on index cards, which were displayed on a card-and-paper trellis for all to view.

They were subsequently collated into booklet form and distributed to all STAR teachers, new and old, to provide a basis for the year of working together. Thus an 'offering' system was adopted, but the strategies came from the teachers.

While this ensured the continued ownership of the scheme on the one hand, any changes in practice were perhaps still grounded within individual styles rather than opening the door to a wider range of styles or a more fundamental shift in primary science practice. This remains a matter for conjecture, however. One outcome was that the teachers who had been presented with a 'ready-made' scheme for the encouragement of process skills were least able to suggest original strategies for other teachers. They declared that, for example, particular strategies to encourage the process skills had been introduced in 1984 and that 'there had been no further change'. In contrast, the teachers in another authority adopted one of these strategies and, together with their children, developed it to have a greater usefulness.

The conference went on to provide training in the observation of science activities. The teachers observed each others' use of process skills while engaged in two extended tasks involving either fire or water. More importantly, they then explored ways of relating the observations to the participants and of building on this information.

Perhaps the most significant and immediate effect of this conference was the recognition by these old STARs that their expertise predated and pioneered the process-based ideas that were by then enshrined in the National Curriculum documents for science. We shall look now at the ways in which the teachers worked with their new STAR colleagues and observed science activities.

PHASE THREE – TEACHERS WORKING TOGETHER

During the third phase of the project both the old and the new STARs worked together. The challenges facing them were numerous, but the main ones can be grouped into four types, namely:

- working with a colleague,
- managing time,
- making classroom observations,
- integrating innovation into existing curriculum policy.

In the following paragraphs, we shall look at these challenges, at the obstacles which cropped up to hinder progress, and at the strategies developed by the STAR teachers to meet the former and overcome the latter. All of the quotations are taken from the termly reports written by the teachers.

The value of this work for anyone trying to fulfil National Curriculum teacher-based assessment requirements was not fully realized until, at the end of the year, the STAR teachers in one authority prepared a booklet (available from the authors) and put on a course entitled 'Exploration of science – strategies for teaching and assessing primary science skills' for forty teachers. It was three times oversubscribed and resulted in some very positive evaluations which will be presented at the end of this chapter.

WORKING WITH A COLLEAGUE

Some of the STAR teachers were experienced team-teachers, but for the majority, planning and teaching *with* another teacher were new experiences. Being observed by a colleague, or having someone observe the children to evaluate one's teaching strategies was not only new, but potentially threatening for many. The first task for the old STARs, therefore, was to establish strategies for working together, and for carrying out and discussing classroom observations without undermining the confidence, status and trust of their new STAR colleagues.

One common strategy was for both teachers to share the task of providing inset for the rest of the staff. In addition to the examples described earlier, other teachers wrote:

> . . . STAR information and activities have been shared by entire staff all the way through . . . this helped greatly because we are no longer uncomfortable about teaching science or being observed . . .   (12)

> . . . we have worked as partners to promote skills to the rest of the staff. As a result their attitudes to science have changed . . .   (13)

Another strategy was for STARs to observe each other, for example:

> . . . we decided to run the lesson between us to help X feel he wasn't being evaluated.   (14)

MANAGING TIME

Problems such as, 'heavy time commitments on both sides' and obstacles such as,

> . . . partner is acting head now so this limits the amount of time available as he is learning the new role . . .   (15)

meant that the best use of the supply cover available had to be carefully planned. In two schools, the headteachers took over one class so that both teachers could plan and discuss the work together, but sufficient time remained a problem for many, as the following comments reveal:

> . . .it was always a problem to find enough time to follow things through *satisfactorily*. Apart from ignoring the children we did not find a good way of overcoming this.   (16)

Sometimes it was helpful if the old STAR did not have a class,

> . . . X floats in and out – we fetch him in when needed.   (17)

but this had some drawbacks too,

> Time was arranged internally as a result of me not being class-based . . . but this meant that my special needs groups did not have my help at these times. (17)

Adequate and uninterrupted time for discussion was difficult to organize, but was essential to make the best use of the supply time which had been made available for teaching and observing each other's children.

> If we arranged things in advance it was easier to have an uninterrupted session, but on a day-to-day referral basis it was hard to meet up.   (18)

> . . .discussion time did not always take place due to unforeseen cover arrangements taking precedence . . . also we found that half-an-hour was too short to arrive at any real conclusions, to take stock and to fully realize the potential of the evaluation.   (19)

It was possible to overcome these problems in some schools, however:

> . . .lesson observed. Followed by discussion about the lesson (children were sent to other classes to give us free time at this stage).   (20)

Team-teaching arrangements eased this problem in some cases:

> Meeting is not a particular problem since we are in a team-teaching situation; formalized meetings are not needed.   (21)

> Even though we work together in an open-plan situation, we need cover in order to work closely together in observing.   (22)

The STAR teachers used their own time to a large extent to overcome the problems of the lack of non-contact time at primary level.

MAKING CLASSROOM OBSERVATIONS

Two strategies were used by many of the teachers to enable them to observe satisfactorily. One was to focus on one skill at a time, and the old STARs began at this stage to consider the quality of a child's utterance, in much the same way as is vital now in order to say which Statement of Attainment best describes a child's performance. As if in anticipation of the need for verbatim evidence, most of the teachers abandoned trying to use the SPOC sheet in the classroom in favour of making freehand notes and relating them to the SPOC categories later. For example:

> One particular skill chosen for observation made it much easier – and written comments instead of just ticks.   (23)

A second major problem encountered was that the children had to have time to get used to their teachers adopting an observing role. The most common way round this was to explain it to them:

> Main difficulty was children trying to watch what I was writing down – most successful strategy was to explain exactly what we were doing, and why. Once they were clear on this point they worked and ignored us.   (23)

Once the children were used to being observed, as in another school which was open-plan, this presented no problem:

. . . our kids are great, if they see you observing they go to other staff.   (24)

At first, when learning what to look for and when finding out what the children do without teacher intervention, a passive approach to observation may be necessary, as one teacher put it:

. . . become part of the furniture – children accept you wandering round. Prepare them well in advance so they can cope without too much interference.   (25)

Once the teacher is familiar with the skills and is quick to recognize examples of them in children's talk and behaviour, observing, assessing and questioning could become part of a minute-by-minute teaching and assessing process. One pair felt that although the role of passive observer was possible:

. . . clearer outcomes seemed to ensue when the observer became more of an active participator – asking questions, creating challenges.   (26)

It was argued that observation is particularly difficult with infants, but one teacher found a way to deal with this by setting a five-minute task such as '. . . find as many things as you can to say about . . .' and capitalizing *immediately* on this time to target one or two groups of children to listen to, before asking all the children to report back. This also gave every child time to think of something to say.

If the children found it difficult to forget the teacher's usual role, some teachers reported finding it difficult to be detached and objective when observing their own children. The writer of the following quote covers a number of the points raised so far, and compares the experience of observing her partner's children with attempting to observe her own:

I changed roles (from teaching to observing) mid-lesson and then monitored the children focusing on one process only – this way of working proved useful but had drawbacks as the children focused on me.

The strategy was therefore modified so that in a second session:

I was the observer. I found it much better. Children focused on X and to a great extent ignored me.

When this was tried in this teacher's own class, however:

I looked at a group and recorded across the columns, but I found it so difficult as could not reach the degree of detachment needed.   (26)

INTEGRATING INNOVATION INTO EXISTING CURRICULUM POLICY

The teachers varied as to whether they saw science as a separate subject, or as an area of experience contributing to cross-curricular themes, but the majority of STAR teachers decided to work on joint topics such as 'gravity', or linked topics, such as 'ourselves' with infants, and 'my body' with juniors. As confidence grew about identifying and providing opportunities to develop process skills within an ever-widening range of content areas, there was a common concern in one authority at least, to integrate science with the rest of the curriculum or make it compatible with school policy:

> . . . we have grown to feel that it is important to avoid science content in isolation – rather to integrate our science into the theme being followed . . . Am increasingly concerned to integrate science within topic work.   (27)

CONCLUSIONS

This chapter is entitled 'Change in teaching primary science'. The results reported in earlier chapters suggest that some limited change was detectable. The criterion adopted for the measurement of change, however, was the most stringent available, namely, the detection of change in children's behaviour in science. It may be that the research plan was over-optimistic in hoping to find a change at that level. Teachers need time to change their attitudes and to internalize a novel approach to science teaching. The STAR teachers felt that their practice had changed as they attempted to provide more opportunities for children to practice process skills. The measure used assumed that the children could use some of those opportunities, and recorded only those which were used. It may have been that the children still needed to learn to use them or to be taught how to use them.

The chapter has reported the teachers' perceptions of change in their practice, the strategies they adopted to facilitate observation and to evaluate change, and has reviewed the phases of the project. In addition, it has provided critical reflection on the decisions made and procedures adopted. Perhaps a longer time span would have led to more change. Perhaps the presentation of a range of models would have broadened the teachers' range of styles and led to more radical change. Perhaps the formal observations should have incorporated a two-year span after all.

At one level however, the original STAR teachers demonstrated considerable professional development by successfully preparing and presenting an in-service day on the assessment of process skills in primary science for forty teachers from the length and breadth of their authority. Overwhelmingly positive evaluations were returned, such as the following typical responses to the question, 'Were there any aspects which you found particularly valuable?'

> The whole day was valuable and I am going to do a condensed re-run for our staff to help them in the way I was helped. The pointers for assessment were invaluable.

> Discussions about implementing science in the busy classroom in terms of recording/assessing.

> Yes, talking to teachers who had had working knowledge of testing . . . it was a stimulating day . . . there must be more courses like this!

To sum up, the fact that the teachers who had devised and tested the strategies also ran the in-service course was obviously much appreciated. The teachers who attended were shown that observation can be used for the assessment of process skills even in 'a busy classroom'. The strategies developed by the STAR teachers overcame many obstacles. It is our intention that this book will share some of those problems and their solutions with other teachers.

Appendix: Science Process Observation Categories (SPOC): Manual for Observers

USING THE SCIENCE PROCESS OBSERVATION CATEGORIES (SPOC)

1. Suggested observation procedures

1.1 Observation intervals are of two minutes, and all the behaviours occurring in each of these intervals are coded, except where stated.

1.2 Pre-selected target pupils are identified and observed in the pre-arranged order, each for two time periods (i.e. four minutes) before passing on to the next. The order of observation of the targets must be randomly selected for each observation visit.

2. Seating of target

Indicate the seating arrangement of the target pupil. If this changes during the observation interval tick the situation which applies for the majority of the time.

Example
A pupil sitting with one other pupil of the same sex would be indicated by ticking 'same sex pair'.

3. Number of children

3.1 *In the classroom*
Write in the number of pupils in the classroom at the time of observation.

3.2 *Involved in science*
Write in the number of pupils who are supposed to be involved in science activities at the time of observation.

4. Coding audience

Audience means person(s) with whom the target is in interaction, whether or not being addressed by the target.

4.1 Thus silent co-operation on a shared task would be coded as having an
to audience, as would the target silently watching a child or group.
4.7 The audience may be an individual pupil, the teacher, a group of two or more pupils, the whole class or none at all.
If an adult other than the teacher is involved, e.g. a parent or ancillary, then code 'OTHER' and specify who.
Only one audience type should be selected for each observation interval. If the audience changes from one to another within the same time interval, code the one which occupies the majority of the time interval.

5. Teacher interaction

Only one category should be ticked, selecting the one which occurs for the majority of the time.

5.1 *Monitoring*
The teacher is monitoring by observing the target pupil or the group or class of which the target pupil is a member.

5.2 *Involved*
The teacher is involved in the interaction in which the target pupil is either engaged or is part of the audience. This could be through class teaching, group teaching, or individual attention.

5.3 *Not present*
The teacher is not involved with the target pupil. He/she might be housekeeping or involved with pupils not in the target pupil's audience.

6. Curriculum area of teacher

Only one curriculum category should be coded for each time interval.
6.1 The teacher's attention may be directed towards 'SCIENCE',
to some 'OTHER' curriculum area, e.g. when group work is taking place,
6.3 some groups may be non-science but have the teacher's attention, or 'NONE', e.g. housekeeping.
If the curriculum area changes during the time interval, code the area which occupied the majority of the time interval.

7. Coding curriculum area (pupil)

7.1   *Only one* curriculum category should be coded for each time interval.
to   The pupil's attention may be directed towards 'SCIENCE', some
7.3   'OTHER' curriculum area, or 'NONE', e.g. in the process of changing task.
If the curriculum area changes during the time interval, code the area which occupied the majority of the time interval.

8. Non-talk activity

8.1   *Making observations*
The target pupil is observing what happens during an event or the reactions of objects, creatures, etc. in test situations. Can also refer to pupils looking at two or more objects, pictures for the purpose of comparison.

Examples
The pupil has a bowl of tap water with a weighted object floating on the surface, and a bowl of salt water with a similar weighted object. The pupil is observing the differences. This may be followed by 'interpretations' or 'hypotheses'.

8.2   *Planning independently*
A child writing or using equipment purposefully in deciding what to do, for planning.

8.3   *Using measuring instruments*
Actively using a measuring device, e.g. rule, litre jug, trundle wheel, scales.

8.4   *Using other materials/equipment*
Actively using materials or equipment other than for measuring, e.g. paper, scissors, sand, water, leaves, shells.

8.5   *Collecting/clearing equipment*
The pupil is collecting or putting away equipment such as scissors, measures, etc., but is not using them.

8.6   *Reading book/worksheet*
The pupil is reading to him/herself from a book or worksheet related to the task. It could be a reference book or book related to a work-scheme.

8.7 *Recording (not copying)*
The pupil is writing or drawing to record what he/she did or learned during an earlier activity. It relates to his own work and is not copied from any source.

8.8 *Copying*
The target pupil is copying from a book, blackboard, worksheets, etc.

8.9 *Waiting for teacher*
The target pupil is waiting to interact with the teacher. He/she might be in a queue or sitting at a table with his/her hand up. Also refers to waiting for the teacher to continue an interaction already started, e.g. in group-teaching a teacher might be interrupted by a non-group pupil. Refers to when the pupil cannot continue with his task until an interaction with the teacher has taken place.

8.10 *Waiting for other pupils*
The target pupil cannot continue with his task until another pupil has done something or interacted with the target, e.g. a construction task may require scissors leaving the target waiting while his/her partner fetches some.

8.11 *Attentive to teacher*
The target pupil is listening to or watching the teacher working on a task related to science.

8.12 *Attentive to other pupils*
The target pupil is listening or watching other pupils working on a science task.

8.13 *Non-attentive to task*
The target pupil is day-dreaming, disruptive, or engaged on activities not related to his task. Includes watching the teacher or a pupil working on a non-science task.

CODING TALK CATEGORIES

For categories 9 and 10 only, three codings are used instead of ticks. For each category, if the target pupil is actively involved, i.e. 'saying' or 'doing' then code '1'. If the target is not *actively* involved but the dialogue is going on in the group of which the target is a member at the time, then code '2'. If both situations occur during the same time interval then code as '1'.

If the dialogue involves the teacher at any time during the observation interval then also code a 'T' for the relevant category.

9. Talk concerning:

    9.1   *Discussing observations*

Refers to description of characteristics of objects or situations which children have directly perceived through their senses. May involve comparisons between objects or events, such as similarities and differences. Includes descriptions of the order in which events took place. Includes descriptions of observations in which a pattern exists ('the biggest went the furthest, then the next biggest and the smallest went the smallest distance') as opposed to a description of the pattern ('the bigger they are the further they go').

Examples

    P.   When you push the blocks down they all float back up.

    T.   Does everyone agree with that . . . when you push them down they all float back up.

    P.   Yes.

    T.   Now, what have you found out that's the same about your blocks?

    P.1   . . . they all float level.

    P.2   . . . they don't dip over . . . like that (gestures with hands).

    T.   That's a lovely observation, anything else . . .?

    T.   Look very closely at the way the blocks float and their weights . . . can you see any pattern there?

    P.   They're all in the same order.

    T.   Can you say anything else . . . can you put that another way?

    T.   What can you tell me about the weight of the block and the way it floated?

    P.   The lightest block floated best . . . and the heaviest block was the worst floater.

    T.   Does everyone agree . . . do you think it has something to do with weight?

    9.2   *Interpretation*

Drawing a conclusion or inference for which there is some (though not necessarily sufficient) evidence in the children's findings. Identifying a pattern linking observations or data. Interpolating or extrapolating from observed data whether or not the pattern which justifies it is stated.

Examples

    T.   Here's a graph showing how fast the soluble aspirin dissolved at different temperatures. Tell me, then, what is the connection between temperature of the water and the time for the aspirin to dissolve?

    P.   As the water gets hotter, the aspirin dissolves quicker.

9.3 *Hypothesizing*
Suggesting an explanation for an event, pattern or finding. It must be more than giving a name ('It's condensation'), possibly taking the form of an associated factor ('It's something to do with air') or a suggested mechanism ('It's because the air gets cold on the side of the can'). It is different from interpretation in that conceptually-based reasons are proposed to account for what is observed. Further evidence is likely to be necessary to test the suggested explanation.

Example
T.   Now why is D the best floater?
P.1 Got more air in it.
P.2 Got more air.
P.3 . . . air bubbles.
(P.1 takes block D out of the water and looks more closely at it.)
P.2 It's lighter.

9.4 *Planning*
This section is concerned with both the general design of the plan (what it is about, what is to be changed, and how any result of that change will be observed), and with discussing specific plans and procedures concerned with carrying out a general plan (how much of this; where does that start from, etc.). This section includes deciding what quantities to use and what to measure and how results are to be observed and measured *but* discussion of the measuring process or the measurements taken are included in 9.6; here the concern is with deciding how they are to be taken.

9.6 *Measurements*
Refers to the discussion of the process of some form of measuring whilst it is taking place, the description of how it was carried out, and the discussion of the measurements subsequently.

Examples
That one looks longer than the other one doesn't it?
It is 7 cm long.
The measure is in millimetres.
Make sure the measure is at the end of the line.

9.7 *Recording*
Refers to discussion about writing notes, taking down results or drawing either during a practical activity or afterwards. Also refers to children talking about the form of record they are making or have made of results. (The content might be reported either as observations or interpretations.)

Examples
Put the title at the top
Write down the measurement. It was 7 cm.
The graph is too small.

9.8   *Raising questions*
Refers to questions about the subject or content of the activity (not interpersonal relations in handling it). Questions which request information, suggest enquiring further, or challenge statements. Not to be confused with hypotheses expressed as questions.

Examples
T.   Are there any other things you would like to find out about balloons?

9.9   *Critical reflection on procedures*
Refers to discussion, usually at the end of an investigation, of different approaches or procedures that could have been used.
Discussing whether and how alternative procedures or changes in those used would have improved the investigation or achieved a better result.

Examples
T.   Is there any way you could make your test better if you did it again?
P.   Well, I could use a different number of turns.
T.   Would that make it better?
P.   Not really.

T.   Do you think you could improve the investigation (of food choice by snails)?
P.   If we'd crushed up the cornflakes it would have been easier to make sure there was the same amount as the other foods. And it would have been fairer.

10. Other talk

10.1   *Recall of previous learning*
Refers to facts, principles, relationships which do not emerge from the current activity, but have to be recalled from memory. Includes names of objects, phenomena, etc., where these words are recalled but not discussed (if they are recalled in order to be discussed the coding 6.4 would be used).

Examples
T.   Does anyone know what this is?
P.   A fossil.

10.2 *Recap of previous activities*
Recap of what was done or found out in a previous lesson, or earlier in the present lesson.

Examples
    T.   What did you find out from your investigation last lesson?
    T.   Did your group do it a different way (last time)?

10.3 *Reading out / discussing instructions*
Refers to the clarification of the task(s) as described orally by the teacher or given in writing. Also to reading out part of written instructions.

Examples
    P.   What does this mean (referring to a written step)?
    T.   responds

    P.   Miss, what are we meant to be writing down?
    T.   responds

    P.   It tells you to weigh them first.

10.4 *Meaning of words*
Refers to the discussion of meaning of words and the clarification of pupil suggestions (as distinct from 1).

Examples
    P.1   They stay up, they don't go right under.
    T.   What's another word we could use to say they stay up?
    P.2   Horizontal.
    T.   Would you agree they all stay horizontal?
           Do you know what we mean by all stay horizontal?
           Show me which way . . .
           . . .so instead of the word level we could have the word horizontal.

10.5 *Asking for help*
The pupil is seeking guidance from the teacher or another pupil about the organization of the task.

Examples
    P.   Where can I find a measuring jug?
    P.   Which shall I do first?

10.6 *Organising task*
Refers to general organization concerned with doing the task such as who will fetch what.

Example
Mary will get the paper while I stick the newspaper.

10.7   *Non-task talk*
This relates to any talk which is not related to the task in any way.

Examples
P.   Did you watch the TV last night?
T.   Put your things away now.

11. Teacher talk

This section is only coded if 'SCIENCE' is the curriculum attention of the teacher, and the teacher is involved with the target pupil or the target's audience.

11.1   *Gives information*
Indicates the teacher has provided facts or information about the content relating to the process or product of the investigations. Includes telling how to use equipment or measuring instruments but not what equipment to use. Can be in the form of a statement or of a question which contains information.

Examples
T.   The name of the force which is slowing down the cars is friction.
T.   You should keep the slope of the ramp the same while you are changing the weight of the cars.
T.   Did you notice how the sugar all dissolved when you stirred the water?

11.2   *Giving instructions*
Refers to teacher instructions about how to carry out an aspect of the task, as distinct from giving information about content. Includes the teacher telling what equipment/materials to use and talk about routine matters related to task supervision.

Examples
T.   So divide your page into two and on the left-hand side say what is the same and on the right-hand side list all the things which are different.
T.   You must read through the worksheets very carefully ... choose one person in your group to be the recorder.

11.3   *Comment on children's answers or actions*
Refers to the teacher's evaluative remarks about the children's responses or about what they are doing and have done.

Examples

    T.   I'm very pleased with your work. You've all worked very scientifically. You have kept to the task but you did carry the experiments further on . . .

11.4   *Asks for account of progress*
Indicates the teacher's request to a pupil, group or whole class to say what they have done or found.

Examples

    T.   How are you getting on.

11.5   *Non-task talk*
Any statements from the teacher which are of a general nature and not specific to the task in hand, e.g. 'Make sure you move your tables back to where they usually are before you leave the room.'

Example

Stop it Wayne, get on with your work.

12. Non-talk teacher activity

This section is only coded if 'SCIENCE' is the curriculum attention of the teacher.

12.1   *Collates pupils' ideas*
The teacher is involved in bringing together ideas or results from several groups or presenting one group's work for others to see. Generally, in whole class context, but could involve a few groups only or even one group where the teacher is acting as a means to help bring results together.

12.2   *Demonstrates activity/what to do*
Teacher carries out part or whole of a practical activity to show how to use the equipment for the particular purpose in hand. May be demonstrated to whole class, group or individual.

12.3   *Listens to pupil(s)*
In general, refers to the teacher listening to pupils talking to each other rather than when in dialogue with the teacher.

12.4   *Reading/writing or collecting pupils' work*
Either at pupils' table or teacher's table, when teacher looks at and may correct children's written work.

PUPIL ID   DATE_____

		1	2	3	4	1	2	3	4	1	2	3	4

1. OBSERVATION FOUND

2. SEATING OF TARGET
- 2.1 alone
- 2.2 same sex pair
- 2.3 mixed sex pair ⓂM
- 2.4 same sex group
- 2.5 mixed sex group
- 2.6 whole class

3. NO OF CHILDREN
- 3.1 in the classroom
- 3.2 involved in science

4. AUDIENCE/INTERACTION
- 4.1 Individual Pupil
- 4.2 Group
- 4.3 Whole Class ⓂM
- 4.4 Teacher
- 4.5 Other (specify)
- 4.6 None

5. TEACHER
- 5.1 Monitoring
- 5.2 Involved ⓂM
- 5.3 Not Present

6. CURRIC.FOCUS OF TCHR
- 6.1 science
- 6.2 other ⓂM
- 6.3 none

7. CURRIC.AREA OF PUP
- 7.1 Science
- 7.2 Other ⓂM
- 7.3 None

8. NON-TALK PUP.ACTIV.
- 8.1 making observations
- 8.2 planning independently
- 8.3 using measuring instruments
- 8.4 using oth.materials/equipt.
- 8.5 collecting,clearing equipt.
- 8.6 reading book/worksheet,etc.
- 8.7 recording (not copying)
- 8.8 copying from bk,wrksht,brd.
- 8.9 waiting for teacher
- 8.10 waiting for oth.pupils
- 8.11 attentive to teacher
- 8.12 attentive to oth.pupils
- 8.13 non-attentive to task
- 8.14 not classifiable

9. DIALOG.INVOLV.PUP.IN
- 9.1 discussing observations
- 9.2 interpretation
- 9.3 hypothesising
- 9.4 general Planning
- 9.5 discuss.specific plans/proc.
- 9.6 measurement
- 9.7 recording
- 9.8 raising questions (for inv.)
- 9.9 critical reflection

10. OTHER PUPIL TALK
- 10.1 recall of previous learning
- 10.2 recap of work done
- 10.3 read out/discuss.instruction
- 10.4 about meaning of words
- 10.5 asking for help
- 10.6 organising task
- 10.7 non-task

11. TEACHER TALK
- 11.1 giving information (task)
- 11.2 giving instructions (task)
- 11.3 comment.on pup's answr(task)
- 11.4 asking for acc. of progress
- 11.5 non-task

12. NON-TLK.TCHR.ACTIV
- 12.1 collat.pupils'.ideas(Brd/OHP)
- 12.2 demonstrat.activ/what to do
- 12.3 listening to pupils
- 12.4 writing on/correct.pups.wrk

NOTES:

ⓂM   denotes majority rule

STAR DAYSHEET

LEA ☐   SCH ☐   CL ☐   DATE ☐☐☐☐☐   AM ☐
                                     PM ☐

PUPIL

☐☐ _____

RESOURCES: _____
_____
_____

EQUIPMENT: _____
_____
_____

TASK DESCRIPTION: _____
_____
_____

PUPIL

☐☐ _____

RESOURCES: _____
_____
_____

EQUIPMENT: _____
_____
_____

TASK DESCRIPTION: _____
_____
_____

PUPIL

☐☐ _____

RESOURCES: _____
_____
_____

EQUIPMENT: _____
_____
_____

TASK DESCRIPTION: _____
_____
_____

PUPIL

▯ ▯ _____

RESOURCES: _____
_____
_____

EQUIPMENT: _____
_____
_____

TASK DESCRIPTION: _____
_____
_____

PUPIL

▯ ▯ _____

RESOURCES: _____
_____
_____

EQUIPMENT: _____
_____
_____

TASK DESCRIPTION: _____
_____
_____

PUPIL

▯ ▯ _____

RESOURCES: _____
_____
_____

EQUIPMENT: _____
_____
_____

TASK DESCRIPTION: _____
_____
_____

OUTLINE OF LESSON

References

Adelman, C. and Walker, R. (1975) *A Guide to Classroom Observation*, Methuen, London.

APU (1980) *Great Britain: Assessment of Performance Unit. DES Primary Survey Number 1*, HMSO, London.

APU (1984) *Great Britain: Assessment of Performance Unit. Science in Schools Research Reports Nos 1, 2 & 3*, HMSO, London.

Barrett, G. (1986) *Starting School: an Evaluation of the Experience*. Final report of an evaluation of reception children to school commissioned by AMMA.

Beckman, L. (1976) Causal attributions of teachers and parents regarding children's performance, *Psychology in Schools*, 13, pp. 212–218.

Bennett, N. (1976) *Teaching Styles and Pupil Progress*. Open Books.

Bennett, N., Desforges, C., Cockburn, A. and Wilkinson, B. (1984) *The Quality of Pupil Learning Experiences*, Lawrence Erlbaum, London.

Bradley, K. (1989) *Great Britain: National Steering Group on the School Teacher Appraisal Pilot Study*.

Burgess, R. (ed.) (1985) *Field Methods in the Study of Education*, Falmer Press, Basingstoke.

Caine, B.S. and Hilsum, S. (1971) *The Teacher's Day*, NFER, Windsor.

Cavendish, S. (1988) *Sex differences related to achievement in mathematics*. Unpublished Ph.D. thesis, University of Leicester.

Cowell, L. (1990) *The Primary Children's Perception of Science*, Unpublished M.Ed. dissertation, University of Leicester.

Croll, P. (1986) *Systematic Classroom Observation*, Falmer Press, Basingstoke.

Delamont, S. (1976) *Interaction in the Classroom*, Methuen, London.

Delamont, S. and Galton, M. (1986) *Inside the Secondary Classroom*, Routledge, London.

DES (1985) *Science 5–16: A Statement of Policy*, HMSO, London.

DES (1989) *Science in the National Curriculum*, HMSO, London.

Edwards, A. and Westgate, D. (1987) *Investigating Classroom Talk*, Falmer Press, Basingstoke.

Eggleston, J., Galton, M. and Jones, M. (1975) *A Science Teacher Observation Schedule, Schools Council Research Series*. MacMillan Educational, London.

Elliott, J. (1976) *Developing Hypotheses about Classrooms from Teachers'*

Practical Constructs. An account of the work of the Ford Teaching Project. North Dakota Study Group on Evaluation. University of North Dakota.

Ennever, L. and Harlen, W. (1972) *With Objectives in Mind. Guide to Science 5/13*. Macdonald Educational, London.

Everton, T. and Impey, G. (eds) (1989) *IT-Inset Partnership in Training*, David Fulton, London.

Fairburn, D. (1988) Pupil Profiling: New Approaches to Recording and Reporting Achievement, in Murphy, R. and Torrance, H. (eds) *The Changing Face of Educational Assessment*, Open University Press, Milton Keynes.

Flanders, N. (1970) *Analyzing Teaching Behaviour*, Addison-Wesley, New York.

Galton, M. (1978) *British Mirrors: A Collection of Classroom Observation Systems*, School of Education, University of Leicester.

Galton, M. (1987a) *Effective Groupwork in the Primary Classroom*, University of Leicester.

Galton, M. (1987b) Structured Observation, in Dunkin, M. (ed.) *The International Encyclopaedia of Teaching and Teacher Education*, Pergamon Press, Oxford.

Galton, M. (1988) The nature of learning in the primary classroom, in Blyth, A. (ed.) *Informal Primary Education Today*, Falmer Press, Basingstoke.

Galton, M. (1989) *Teaching in the Primary School*. David Fulton, London.

Galton, M. and Simon, B. (eds) (1980) *Progress and Performance in the Primary Classroom*, Routledge and Kegan Paul, London.

Galton, M., Simon, B. and Croll, P. (1980) *Inside the Primary Classroom*, Routledge, London.

Galton, M. and Delamont, S. (1985) Speaking with a forked tongue? Two styles of observation in the ORACLE project, in R. Burgess (ed.) *op. cit.*

Galton, M. and Patrick, H. (eds) (1990) *Curriculum Provision in the Small Primary School*, Routledge, London.

Harlen, W. *et. al.* (1977) *Schools Council: Progress in Learning Science Project*, MacMillan Publications, London.

Harlen, W. (1985) *Teaching and Learning Primary Science*. Paul Chapman Publishing, London.

Harlen, W. (1986) *Planning scientific investigations at age 11. Science report for teachers No. 8*, published by the ASE for the DES.

Harlen, W. and Jelly, S. (1989) *Developing Science in the Primary Classroom*, Oliver and Boyd, Edinburgh.

Hart, K. (1981) *Children's Understanding of Mathematics, 11–16*, Murray, London.

Holt, M. (1981) *Evaluating the Evaluators*, Hodder and Stoughton, Sevenoaks.

Holt, J. (1964) *How Children Fail*, Pitman, New York.

Hilsum, S. and Cane, B. (1971) *The Teacher's Day*, NFER, Slough.

Jelly, S. (1985) Helping children to raise questions – and answering them, in Harlen, W. (ed.) *Primary Science: Taking the Plunge*, Heinemann, London.

Joyce, B. and Weil, M. (1986) *Models of Teaching* (3rd edn), Prentice-Hall International Editions, Hemel Hempstead.

Kuhn, D., Amsel, E. and O'Laughlin, M. (1988) *The Development of Scientific*

Thinking Skills, Academic Press, New York.

National Curriculum Council (1989) *Science Non-Statutory Guidance*, NCC, York.

Pollard, A. (1985) *The Social World of the Primary School*, Holt, Rinehart and Winston, London.

Pollard, A. (ed.) (1987) *Children and their Primary Schools*, Falmer Press, Basingstoke.

Powell, J. (1985) *The Teacher's Craft*, SCRE Publication.

Rosenshine, B. (1980) How time is spent in elementary classrooms, in Denham, C. and Lieverman, A. (eds) *Time to Learn*, Department of Health Education and Welfare, National Institute of Education, Washington DC.

Rosenshine, B. (1987) Direct Instruction in Dunkin, M. (ed.) *Teaching and Teacher Education*, Pergamon Press, Oxford.

Rosenshine, B. and Furst, N. (1973) The use of direct observation to study teaching, in Travers, R. (ed.) *Second Handbook of Research on Teaching*, Rand McNally, Chicago.

Rowe, M. B. (1974) Wait time and rewards as instructional variable, their influence on languages, logic and fate control, *Journal of Research in Science Teaching*, Vol. 7, pp. 81–94.

Rowlands, S. (1988) An interpretative model of teaching and learning, in Pollard, A. (ed.) *op. cit.*

Russell, T. and Harlen W. (1990) *Assessing Science in the Primary Classroom: Practical Tasks*, Paul Chapman Publishing, London.

Sanger, J. (1988) Classroom observation workshops and the ethics of perception, *Cambridge Journal of Education*, Vol. 18, no. 3, pp. 287–296.

Schilling, M. D., Hargreaves, L., Harlen, W., with Russell, T. (1990) *Assessing Science in the Primary Classroom: Written Tasks*, Paul Chapman Publishing, London.

Schools Council (1977) see Harlen, W. *op. cit*

Sheal, P. (1989) Classroom observation: training the observers, *English Language Teaching Journal*, Vol. 43, no. 2, pp. 92–103.

Simon, A and Boyer, E. (eds.) (1970) *Mirrors for Behaviour: An Anthology of Classroom Observation Instruments*, Research for Better Schools, Philadelphia.

Spooner, R. (1980) Teacher Craft: a review of Focus on Teaching by Bennett, N. and McNamara, D. (eds), *Education*, June 27th.

TGAT (1987) *National Curriculum Task Group on Assessment and Testing. A Report*, DES.

Tobin, K. (1984) Student task involvement in activity oriented science, *Journal of Research in Science Teaching*, Vol. 21, no. 5, pp. 469–82.

Walker, R. and Wiedel, J. (1985) Using photographs in a discipline of words. In Burgess, R. (ed.) *op. cit.*

Williams, M. (1989) A developmental view of classroom observations, *English Language Teaching Journal*, Vol. 43, no. 2, pp. 85–91.

Woods, P. (1989a) *How Children Think and Learn*, Basil Blackwell, Oxford.

Woods, P. (1988) *Working for Teacher Development*, Report on the Records of Achievement Pilot Study.

Index